D1594517

Letters from Cairo

Arab American Writing

Other titles in Arab American Writing

The Cairo House: A Novel
    Samia Serageldin

A Community of Many Worlds: Arab Americans in New York City
    The Museum of the City of New York

Hayati, My Life: A Novel
    miriam cooke

Post Gibran: Anthology of New Arab American Writing
    Munir Akash and Khaled Mattawa, eds.

The Situe Stories
    Frances Khirallah Noble

Letters from Cairo

PAULINE KALDAS

Syracuse University Press

First Edition 2007
07 08 09 10 11 12   6 5 4 3 2 1

The paper used in this publication meets the minimum requirements of
American National Standard for Information Sciences—Permanence of
Paper for Printed Library Materials, ANSI Z39.48–1984.∞™

For a listing of books published and distributed by Syracuse University Press,
visit our Web site at SyracuseUniversityPress.syr.edu.

ISBN-13: 978-0-8156-0854-7
ISBN-10: 0-8156-0854-3

Library of Congress Cataloging-in-Publication Data
Kaldas, Pauline, 1961–
Letters from Cairo / Pauline Kaldas.—1st ed.
p. cm.—(Arab American writing)
Includes bibliographical references.
ISBN-13: 978–0–8156–0854–7 (hardcover : alk. paper)
ISBN-10: 0–8156–0854–3 (hardcover : alk. paper)
1. Egypt—Social life and customs. 2. Egypt—Description and travel. 3. Kaldas, Pauline,
1961——Travel—Egypt. 4. Kaldas, Pauline, 1961—Family. I. Title.
DT70.K27 2006
962.05—dc22   2006038967

Printed in China through Four Colour Imports, Ltd., Louisville, Kentucky

For my parents,
who had the courage to begin a new life;

for my daughters,
Yasmine and Celine, the future;

and for my husband,
T. J., who made this journey possible.

Pauline Kaldas was born in Egypt and immigrated with her parents to the United States at the age of eight in 1969. She is the author of *Egyptian Compass,* a collection of poetry, and the coeditor of *Dinarzad's Children: An Anthology of Contemporary Arab American Fiction.* Her poetry, fiction, and nonfiction have appeared in a variety of journals and anthologies. She received her Ph.D. from Binghamton University and currently teaches at Hollins University in Roanoke, Virginia.

Contents

Illustrations

Acknowledgments

First and foremost, I would like to thank the Hollins University community, especially our faculty colleagues, who supported us as we made this trip and whose response to my initial letters encouraged me to complete this book. Special thanks to Provost Wayne Markert, who understood that this was a "family project" and made it possible for all of us to go to Egypt. This book was supported in part by a grant from Hollins University.

My great appreciation goes to Community School, which sent our daughters off with great farewell parties and welcomed them back with open arms. Special thanks to all their teachers and especially Laurie Beck, the director of Community School.

I extend my love and thanks to my family and to my husband's family for their support and understanding as we make our journeys. My gratitude also goes to my extended family in Egypt, who welcome me back each time I return.

I am especially grateful to those who read various drafts of the manuscript and offered excellent suggestions for improving it: Michelle Abate, T. J. Anderson III, and Alyssa Antonelli. Additional thanks to those who helped with this project in a variety of ways, especially Andreas Alexandrou, Jeffner Allen, Maggie Awadallah, Jean Fallon, Ayman Al Kharrat, Lisa Suhair Majaj, and Mona Sarkiss.

My heartfelt thanks go to Cherry Chapman, who guided me through the creation of the painting that is now on the cover of this book. I also express my deepest appreciation to Renee Godard, who encouraged me to take Cherry's art class.

I am also fortunate to have such extraordinary daughters who help me to see the world in a new way.

Journeys

Journeys

In January 2002, my husband, T. J. Anderson III, an African American poet and scholar, was awarded a six-month Fulbright grant to teach American literature at Cairo University and to research jazz music in Egypt. We were both teaching at Hollins University, a small women's college in Southwest Virginia. Our two daughters were attending Community School, an independent school with an innovative curriculum. When T. J. accepted the Fulbright, we looked forward to our trip with excitement and some apprehension.

I was born in Egypt, and my parents and I immigrated to the United States in 1969. My parents' decision to immigrate was influenced by various economic, religious, and political factors. Until the mid-1960s, immigration restrictions were strict, and it was rare for Egyptians to immigrate. In 1965, the United States passed a less restrictive act that favored those with certain jobs, including engineering, which happened to be my father's profession. Egypt's defeat in the 1967 war with Israel also caused many Egyptians to look elsewhere for opportunities to improve their lives. A large number of Egyptians immigrated in the 1960s and 1970s, and that period has come to be known in Egypt as the "brain drain." Many of those who chose to immigrate were Coptic Orthodox Christians like my own family. Copts are a religious minority in Egypt and, like other minorities, they have been subject to discrimination and limited opportunities. When we arrived in Boston, there were about ten Coptic families who used to get together, and they eventually began a church. Today, the Coptic

Orthodox Church in Boston has a membership of over six hundred families.

My parents applied for immigration to Canada and the United States. They were accepted to both countries, and I vaguely remember having to accompany them on interviews where someone who seemed to have great authority sat behind a desk and asked them questions. My parents decided to go to the United States, perhaps because one of my mother's cousins and her husband had already immigrated to California, and so our tickets were to take us to Los Angeles. However, my mother has told me the story of how our destination changed by coincidence. Several months before we were to leave, my mother was standing in line at Cairo University to get her transcripts. She heard the name of a distant cousin being called. It was a cousin that she had never met but she recognized the name, so she found her and introduced herself. As they began to talk, my mother discovered that her cousin, Phoebe, and her husband were immigrating to the States about six months before us. Their destination was Boston, and Phoebe convinced my mother that we should stop to see them before we headed to California. When we arrived in Boston, my mother fell in love with the city and wanted to stay. So she and my father struck a bargain: if they could both find work within a week, they would stay, and if they couldn't, they would go on to California. My parents set off on Monday with the addresses of several companies. They got off the subway together and went in different directions, agreeing to meet at the end of the day. My mother was particularly apprehensive because she had never worked in Egypt. By the end of that day, they had both been offered jobs. My mother found a position in an insurance company, and my father found two jobs, one in an engineering company and one in an architectural firm. And so we settled in Boston.

I was eight and a half years old when we immigrated. Leaving the only home I had known was difficult, particularly because my childhood was filled with the nurturing of an extended family. In Egypt, my parents and I lived with my grandmother and aunt, and each week my cousins would come over or we would go to visit. Despite being an only child, I never felt lonely. Immigration brought with it the isolation that came as a result of moving away from the extended family.

We went to Egypt for a brief visit in 1976, a trip that reawakened my desire to return at some point. That opportunity came in 1990 when I applied for a position at the American University in Cairo (AUC) and was hired to teach in the Freshman Writing Program. I had just gotten married, and so T. J. and I prepared for our new adventure. In some ways, I was more nervous than he was, wondering if I would be able to fit in, to become Egyptian again. Perhaps I also feared that the reality of Egypt would contradict the nostalgia of my childhood memories.

We spent three years in Egypt, both of us teaching at the American University in Cairo. At AUC we found a supportive expatriate community. We made new friends and became involved in the challenge of teaching students whose lives straddled two cultures. I also reunited with my extended family, finding it easier than I had anticipated to slip back into my place. T. J. discovered that his brown skin and African American features allowed him to blend in easily. Egyptians told him that he had classic Egyptian features and insisted that his ancestry must be Egyptian. Perhaps that is what allowed him to connect so easily to the culture and feel a sense of belonging. My family embraced both of us, and I was able to regain the nurturing of that extended family. Our first daughter, Yasmine, was born in Egypt, just one week before our return to the United States in 1993. We left Egypt to attend graduate school at Binghamton University in upstate New York. It was a place that we grew to love as our family continued to expand. In the middle of our graduate school years, our second daughter, Celine, was born in Binghamton in 1996.

As our daughters grew, my urge to return to Egypt increased. To them, relatives in Egypt were just names that they easily forgot, foods like *kosharee* and *taamia* were just strange words rather than a distinct taste on their tongues, and the landscape of Cairo was only pictures of pyramids, not the energy of a city in constant movement. I wanted their first trip outside of the United States to be to Egypt. I wanted them to know the country of their origin not through stories and pictures, but through the reality of being physically there. I wanted them to know their distant cousins and aunts and uncles, to know that their history extended far back and that they were part of a family that spanned two continents.

The Fulbright offered us the opportunity to return, this time with our children. How they would experience Egypt and whether or not they would be able to adjust to a different culture was what made me apprehensive. What I did not know when we set off is that their presence would allow me to reexperience my native country through their eyes, that I would see it again as if for the first time, and that I would see not only further back in time but also forward into an unknown future.

While we were in Egypt, I wrote six letters back to friends and family. It was a way to share our experiences with those who had given us so much support. Perhaps it was also a way of bearing witness, of recording our experiences and observations at that particular time. The positive comments I received in response to my letters encouraged me to put together this book. At the heart of it are those six letters. In addition, there are e-mails, poems, and pictures by my daughters, Yasmine and Celine, excerpts from my journal, recipes of some of our favorite foods, and reflections that I wrote after we returned, as well as essays based on earlier visits to Egypt. It is the collage of our journey.

My Home

The Palm trees are swaying gently
The River is flowing softly
And on the other side of the world is my home.

Yasmine Aida Kaldas Anderson

Journal Entries

January 25

I'm making circles again, moving towards destinations that become points of departure, holding two homes till it seems my only place of comfort is in transit. Moving through airports for the last two days: Roanoke, Detroit, Amsterdam, Cairo—I'm reminded of how large the world is, of the variety of those who live in it, of how in the creation of these airports and the ability to cross borders, we encapsulate it—how much of the world is held in a single international airport.

In the Amsterdam airport, I look around at others who are headed to Egypt: the young Egyptian couple whose son is crying—are they returning home to Egypt or just visiting? The tall, slender woman with long blond hair sitting with an Egyptian man and two boys who look like their father—where is she from and how did this become her life? The young Egyptian man who was on the previous flight with us reading an Arabic book and who now walks into the terminal carrying a McDonald's bag—who is he and where is he going? Then my glance turns inward: we're an Egyptian-looking family speaking English, and I know the man across from us is wondering who we are.

I had been dreading this trip, wondering if urging T. J. to apply for the Fulbright and bring us here was a mistake, a moment of nostalgic insanity. Then after T. J. accepted the Fulbright, 9/11 happened. Besides our own concerns, we had to contend with other people questioning our decision to go to the Middle East. What we had anticipated as a positive journey began to make us anxious and uncertain.

Now as each step brings us closer, my fears disappear. Once out of the dirt, concrete, and pressure of the Cairo airport, I breathe deeply. And Yasmine comments on the trees, the bits of greenery she didn't expect to see. Celine is still worried about being able to speak to people, but I know everything will be fine now.

We drive to Zamalek at two in the morning, our suitcases dragging the car as the rag the driver tore into three pieces and tied into a rope to keep the trunk closed strains against every bump in the road. I'm breathing in the dust air as if it were the breath of a jasmine flower. I'm home with that urge to bend and kiss the ground—but perhaps more distant this time. I feel more American at this point in my life than I have before. We adapt despite our will. It is Yasmine and Celine who have pulled me into America in a way I could never have accomplished myself. At some point we must claim things as our own. At the age of forty, I have claimed America as home and the loss of homeland is less painful. So, returning here this time feels more joyous, not so encumbered by the pain of the past.

Yet, my trip to Egypt began in the Roanoke airport when I beeped going through security. Pulled aside behind a curtain, a woman ran her metal detector and then her hands down and across my body, politely asking if I minded. I cooperated, offering the luggage keys. When she was done, and the other woman who had been standing there left, she asked in Arabic if I was Arab. Focusing on the tension of the moment, I hadn't noticed her full features until she spoke. "Yes," I answered. "I thought so," she said, "That's why I brought you here behind the curtain." "Where are you from?" I asked. "I'm Palestinian," she answered. And I smiled to embrace our connection, realizing that we are everywhere, and that Arab American is not a fragmented identity but one that is whole and that we create. It is an identity that becomes transformed through immigration in this new place where the need for unity is greater than the issues that divide us. In Egypt, I learned how accents, clothing, religion, and politics differentiate us; our uniqueness is created in part by highlighting those differences. We bring our distinctive national identities with us to the United States, yet the similarities of language and cultural origin pull us toward each other to create an Arab American identity, enabling us to acknowledge that here we belong together.

So we're in this temporary apartment that none of us like because it's old and dusty. T. J. is worried about the Fulbright and teaching at Cairo University. And Yasmine is anxious and tearful about the unfamiliarity. And Celine's ears hurt on the plane coming down and kept hurting as she cried in the airport. But, as she says, "It's good to cry because it makes the sadness come out."

Once Yasmine finished exploring the dark rooms of the apartment, she sat down to read a book, making everything around her disappear. She's eight and a half years old, almost exactly as old as I was when I immigrated to America. But for her this is temporary, and her life in America waits for her return. Celine has just recently turned five. She's at the beginning of gathering memories and being able to hold them permanently.

Now it's 2:15 in the afternoon. I was awakened at noon by the voices outside, the cars honking, and a cat meowing. Everyone else is still sleeping and I had better wake them.

January 26

We went to bed last night at 10:30, but Celine woke us up at two in the morning and kept us up until about 5:00. She kept talking about Community School and her friends and how much she missed them. Then Yasmine started listing all the friends she missed. For them, I know these first days are hard when the unfamiliarity of Egypt stings so tangibly.

There's a magnolia tree right outside the window here like the one outside our window in Virginia. Looking at it, I feel that I exist firmly balanced.

January 27

Yasmine has a stomachache, and Celine seems to have a cold and trouble breathing. I'm sure it's because of the dust. I feel bad bringing them to a place so polluted. If only we could choose our own homeland, I'd choose some place clean and pretty. But once born, so much is imprinted on us.

Yesterday, we ate at the Marriott Hotel, which is in Zamalek near the British School. Security guards hover around as people and cars enter, and to get inside the building we had to go through a metal detector and the scrutiny of two officers who searched our bags. It is clear that the Marriott doesn't simply rely on foreigners and tourists for its business. Inside, the garden restaurant is filled with upper-class Egyptians. Unlike most of the women on the streets of Cairo who dress conservatively, the women at the Marriott wear their hair loose, and their tight fitting clothes clearly display their bodies. Everyone walks as if they were on a runway. As T. J. reminds us, "They're here to see and to be seen." The discrepancy between rich and poor, with the rich marked by Western modernism, has become even more striking.

So today, a woman hired by Fulbright came to clean the apartment. She has two sons who graduated from college. One has a simple job and the other is unemployed and eager to come to America. "And is America nice?" she asked me. "Yes, but it's hard," was the simplest answer I could give that came close to truth.

January 31

Difficult—everything—so much energy expended on small things. We have finally moved into another apartment. All of us like this apartment much better. It's clean, and the rugs and furniture are new. We've almost unpacked, and we've gone to the supermarket and have most of our basics. Now we're on the other side of Zamalek so we have to become familiar with what's around us.

A Border Crossing: 1969

My clearest memory is of my grandmother touching my face with her hand to wake me up at five o'clock in the morning. My cousins were asleep on the floor at the foot of the bed. The rest of the relatives—more cousins, aunts, uncles, grandparents, great aunts and uncles—were scattered throughout the apartment sleeping on beds, sofas, the floor, wherever there was space. Those who couldn't spend the night arrived early in the morning. We had been told to get to the airport several hours before the flight, and everyone wanted to see us off.

My cousin Usama and I had devised a plan. I was to find a secret hiding place: we had decided on under the bed. He was to keep them from finding me; they would have to leave without me so they could catch the plane. But it didn't work. When I went to hide, he just stood there numb and did nothing as they found me. Years later, when I saw him, he looked at me and said, "What are you? You're not Egyptian. You're not American." I wanted to tell him that he had betrayed our pact that morning, that it was his fault too.

I don't remember much about getting dressed or eating, only that it was probably my grandmother who got me ready. When I had asked her about America, she could only tell me that it was very cold there and I would have to wear many layers of warm clothes. Years later, I had decided to leave my family in Boston and go to graduate school. Sitting in the car with my father, I broke our usual silence and told him I was going to Michigan. His only response was to say, "You know, it's very cold there."

At the airport, I clung tightly to my grandmother refusing to let go, and they had to pull me from her. Our whole family was there, and other people stared at us. With our crying, hugging, and shouting, we had become a spectacle. Now when I go to Egypt, I make sure my family doesn't know when I'm arriving or leaving and I settle for a taxi ride. On the plane leaving Egypt, my parents tried to cheer me up by giving me the window seat but I sat there crying. I tried to formulate my feelings, to identify the things I would miss: my grandmother, my cousin, and my dog, Rita. But every time I thought of them, I would start crying again. My mother has often reminded me that I cried all the way to Vienna. We had a layover there and we saw snow for the first time. I had to give up my black patent leather Egyptian shoes for a pair of tight zippered boots.

We had another stopover in London, and we stayed there for a few days. I remember going to a department store with my parents and waiting while they bought some blankets. I overheard some girls speaking English, their words quick and eruptive. It didn't sound anything like the English I had learned in school. Later, when I entered fourth grade in America, I kept trying to speak Arabic to my classmates, thinking they should be able to understand me.

We arrived in Boston on December 24, 1969, Christmas Eve, except it wasn't Christmas in Egypt since Coptic Christmas is on January 7. The next day we took a walk through the park in Harvard Square with my distant aunt and uncle who had arrived just six months before us. Everyone laughed as my aunt kept falling in the snow, unable to steady her footing. Someone took a picture of us, and I saw myself bundled up in my Egyptian coat looking sullen and angry while everyone else was smiling. When I got my Christmas present that year, a red plastic telephone, I used it to pretend I was calling Egypt.

The date 1969 has become so etched in my mind that sometimes I mistakenly put it down as my birth date. I was eight years old when we immigrated. Looking back, I realize how delicate a child is at that age. We still respond to everything instinctively and emotionally, yet our intellect is beginning to form and the two have just started to intersect.

On the first day of school, my mother asked the neighbor's two daughters to walk with me and wait for me afterwards. At the end of the day, I looked in vain for them. Then I gave up and tried to find my own way home. I got terribly lost and when I finally had the courage to ask someone, they couldn't understand my accent. So I just kept walking and what was probably a ten-minute walk took me hours.

Sometimes when the world around me seems so distant, as if there is nowhere for me to place my steps, I pretend I'm still asleep in bed. My grandmother hasn't touched my face yet, and I have only been dreaming my new life in America.

February 2002

Letter 1: February 2002

Dear Family and Friends,

Every morning I wake to the voices of children shouting and playing at the school right across the street from our building. They begin around 7:30 with an incongruous harmony of songs and responses to the lead teacher who conducts their energetic voices. The noise subsides until 1:30 in the afternoon, when they let out for the day, clamoring to the kiosks that sell candy and the carts full of steaming peanuts and pumpkin seeds.

We are living on 26A Bahgat Ali Street in Zamalek. Zamalek is actually a large island in the middle of the Nile River. Like much of Cairo, it's congested with traffic, people, and stores. The streets are filled with noise here: people speaking, shouting, or selling. And the cars and taxis constantly honk their horns, sometimes to warn another car or pedestrian of their presence, other times simply to assert a right to their piece of the road.

Human interaction is constant here beginning the moment we step out of the building with the *bawab* (doorman) greeting us. Yasmine and Celine have become quite good at saying *sabah el kheir* (good morning). Then we have to walk on the sidewalks which look like they were put together out of mismatched jigsaw pieces made of broken concrete and dirt. Uneven and littered, it takes both concentration and imagination to walk in this city. And just when you think you've found an even stretch to walk on, there will be a car parked right on the sidewalk, and you have to go around it onto the street where cars are double-parked. Then you have to try to maintain that centimeter of space between your body and the passing traffic. I have described walking here as a dance to Yasmine, and so she pliés and pirouettes her way through the streets quite gracefully. Celine steps along calmly, seemingly oblivious to anything out of the ordinary.

The apartment we finally moved into (different from the one we were promised) is quite nice. It has two bedrooms, one and a half bathrooms, and a spacious kitchen with a table and chairs, unlike most kitchens here that are tiny and cramped. There is a dining room and two living rooms, or reception areas, as they are called. And there is the balcony giving us a view of the various apartment buildings and hotels, along with a wonderful picture of the city skyline. We have air conditioners and heaters, items which were a rarity when we were here nine years ago. And we even have a washing machine, but dryers are still difficult to find and very expensive so we hang our clothes up on the balcony.

Our TV has about five channels, with one providing English and French programs. Watching the news here has been an exercise in shifting perspectives. Every newscast, regardless of whether it is in Arabic, French, or English, begins with news of Palestine and Israel, first highlighting Israeli attacks and the number of Palestinians killed. The images of the violence are far more graphic than anything we get in the States. I'm constantly made aware of the degree to which the media shapes our understanding of current events as well as our judgments of the actions of other countries. World News also receives more coverage here, with special segments on news in Africa and in Asia.

The store shelves are loaded with Western products from soaps and shampoos to coffee makers and computers. Celine found her gummy bears and Yasmine found the Harry Potter books, and the first Harry Potter movie is even playing at one of the hotels. Because of the inundation of Western products and the negative effect on the Egyptian economy, a recent law has restricted the amount of foreign goods, especially new clothing, which people can bring into the country. In response to an interview about this law in a local magazine, a *bawab* responded, saying, "Who the hell cares? I have two galabeyas. One for summer, and the other for winter. And I don't know where the airport is. What's wrong with *kastour* [cheap quality fabric]? It still covers your private parts, doesn't it?"

Western products are perceived to be superior to anything made in Egypt and of course they're very expensive. The cost of living has gone way up, making the poor even poorer while the middle class scrambles even more to make ends meet. Yet, there is still a strong upper class. The upscale restaurants and hotels are crowded with Egyptians, wearing the latest styles and flashing their mobile phones like jewelry. These are the same people whom you rarely see walking on the streets because they have cars and drivers (no wonder their shoes look so good; mine were ruined after two weeks). And they vacation in villas by the Red Sea or abroad bringing back dollars that are now highly sought after because the exchange rate is 4.5 pounds to the dollar. On the black market, it can go up to six pounds.

T. J. has begun teaching at Cairo University. His first task was proving his American identity. No one here believes he is not Egyptian, not only because he is African American with a similar complexion, but also because many Egyptians assume that all Americans are white and blond. T. J. is constantly asked if his parents are Egyptian, his grandparents, and so on. He has been told on many occasions that his appearance as well as his mannerisms and gestures are those of a typical Egyptian. After a few days, word got around the university and now his identity is well known. He is teaching two courses in Practical Criticism. He has discovered that British literature continues to dominate the curriculum in the English Department. In particular, the poetry taught is very traditional with set rhyme schemes. Although some students have a strong interest in multicultural American literature, they are introduced to little of it in the classroom. However, he has also been fortunate in meeting several colleagues who are willing to move beyond tradition and introduce students to a broader range of literature. He has become known as Thomas since T. J. doesn't make sense here and is too complicated to explain. He wears a jacket and tie every day and, as he says, no one at Hollins University would recognize him now.

Celine has started school at Stepping Stones, a preschool that has a kindergarten class (here called KG1). It is an English language school that is supposedly American run. I don't think she is learning much in the way of academics, but she has a nice teacher and the field trips are good. She is particularly enjoying her karate class, which I fear she might have reason to use given some of the boys in the school. There are three girls in her class with whom she has become friends: Nada, Habiba, and Yoki. She gets to wear a uniform and the teachers like to put her hair in a ponytail. She is beginning to look quite like an Egyptian schoolgirl.

Side note: The Egyptian economy may be as mysterious to explain as how the pyramids were built. When I went to look at Celine's school, the director told me the fees were 700 pounds per month plus 100 pounds for the registration fee. A few days later, when I went to pay the registration fee, the director wasn't there, so I spoke to the secretary who told me the fees were 250 dollars per month (about 100 dollars more than what the director said). When I explained that the director had said 700, the secretary said that was fine. Then on the first day of school when I wanted to pay for the first month, there was no secretary or director, so I spoke to the accountant who told me the fees were 850 pounds per month. Again, I explained, and he said it was fine to pay only 700. Well, I guess it all goes along with having to give a tip to the man who slices your cheese and luncheon meat at the supermarket, and the salesperson who shows you merchandise in a shop, as well as the one who wraps your pastries, and of course the one who mysteriously appears from behind the Queen's Pyramid in Giza to give you a tour.

Yasmine will start school at the beginning of March at the Pakistan International School when a new term will begin. The school has a very international student body and the language of instruction is English. It's a small school, a bit chaotic, but the students and teachers seem quite nice. While waiting for school to start, she has been reading voraciously. She finished all the books we brought with us and we had to make an urgent trip to an English language bookstore.

Side note: I've learned a great deal while trying to find a school for Yasmine. First I visited the East Language International School, which was very eager to take her. While I tried to keep an open mind, the lack of cleanliness made me very uneasy. Although it's an English-language school, all the signs in the classroom were in Arabic. Then there was the British International School where it cost us 150 dollars to have Yasmine take the entrance exams. The school has excellent facilities and a strong academic program. Finally, they accepted Yasmine, but the director said she would have to be in a lower grade because "she hasn't been through the British system." When I was a child in Egypt, I attended an English-language school; at the time, I believe, those were the most sought after schools. When I was teaching at the American University in Cairo in the early 1990s, those students who had come through the French schools seemed to be the most favored. Recently, I have been hearing that the German schools are becoming the most competitive. The importance of elementary and secondary education is apparent given that people include the schools they attended on their résumés, and employers take note of them when making hiring decisions. I've heard stories of parents going to great lengths to enroll their children in the most prestigious international schools.

I think I'm the one having the most difficult time adjusting. Maybe it's because I always expect to feel a sense of belonging but instead find myself ill at ease. People know I'm Egyptian, but they sense that something isn't quite right by the way I speak and move. So I feel far more American here than I do in the States. I'm beginning to think I can only belong on a plane between both countries, suspended in flight. Still, I'm glad to be here again, especially to see my family where I do belong, where I have a place that connects me to others in a way that no distance can break. And I can hear Arabic spoken again, and shouted, that disharmony of voices in a place alive and spirited where I can still walk. We miss you all, Pauline (known here as Lina)

Journal Entries

February 6

Went to Garden City yesterday—the man who owns the watch shop remembered us from eight years ago, the men in the grocery store smiled with recognition, and the man in the pastry shop also remembered. Here, if you go to the same store, you establish a relationship; a bond is formed and its strength holds. But in the U.S., I can go to the supermarket everyday and my presence will remain irrelevant. The man who used to wrap our pastries in Tseppas and who used to tell me he wanted to go to America died six months ago. His name was Mustafa—died of cancer, still in his forties. The new man in Tseppas who helped us said America was a racist country with no morals. And another man said everyone with black hair is now suspect in America. Mustafa must have died before 9/11, his vision of America still intact.

February 8

Took a taxi to the book fair, which I found out had closed on Monday. I was disappointed since the book fair is a major event where books from all over the world are sold and thousands of people attend. Instead, I had a long talk with the cab driver who took me to a kiosk downtown where I found all the Arabic posters and books I wanted to get at the book fair. Everyone wants to talk about America and 9/11. This cab driver told me people are angry at the way the U.S. tries to dictate to other countries. People are fed up, he said, with the way the U.S. handles the Palestinian issues and how it wants everyone to accept America's right to defend itself but won't allow other countries, especially Palestine, to do the same. He argued that in response to the terrorist acts of 9/11, the U.S. destroyed a whole country, but it won't let Palestine do anything. Then he told me this story to demonstrate how terrorism is born:

> *There was an officer walking in the street and there was a poor woman selling things on the sidewalk. Next to her was her thirteen-year-old son. The officer walked by her and turned over her items, destroying them. The woman could do nothing. Her son watched helpless as his mother was humiliated and her goods were lost. A vein opened inside his body as he stood helpless and unable to act. Years later, the officer had become the chief officer and he was still walking down the streets doing the same thing. But this time it was the woman's grown son who was selling on the sidewalk. When he saw the chief officer, he picked up a banana cutter and killed him. Because what he saw done to his mother had stayed with him and opened a vein in his body.*

February 13

Five in the morning—can't sleep. Celine kicking off the covers and Yasmine complaining. And I'm worried about more things than I can count—my eyelids swollen and itchy maybe from those flowers I bought yesterday or whatever they might be sprayed with; thinking I need to call the American University in Cairo to find out about a job but wondering if it's a good idea to work; wishing we had just come here for a vacation; upset that we haven't shown the kids more at this point; and frustrated that we haven't gotten into a routine and our days still feel unsettled.

Life here is constant contact with people, at times reassuring and at other times exhausting. And everywhere people ask me what is America like now after 9/11, and I'm not sure what to say except that there are good people in America—I have one foot on each continent and I can't seem to strike a balance. I look at Yasmine and Celine and realize how American they are. Let them forge ahead, create something new. I hope they will never feel the loss I have known.

February Reflection

A SENSE OF PLACE

Zamalek

The island of Zamalek is a busy, bustling place with tall apartment buildings rising into the sky and streets dotted with restaurants, small grocery stores, and kiosks. The main roads travel the length and width of the island while the smaller streets wiggle their way through narrower sections. When the school day ends, an abundance of children pour out taking over the sidewalks and streets. Zamalek is not so different from other parts of Cairo like Garden City, where we lived from 1990 to 1993. But as I walked the streets of this island in the six months we lived there, I tried to imagine a different Zamalek—the one that existed when Egypt was colonized by the British. I am told that this is where most of the British lived. They built large villas with spacious gardens, creating for themselves an oasis in the midst of their new colony. It was probably a part of the city that few Egyptians entered. Egypt gained its final independence from Britain in 1952, but for a long time Zamalek remained a place inhabited by foreigners and the wealthy. Today, only a few villas dot the cramped streets of Zamalek, and almost all of those have become schools, embassies, or homes to ambassadors. Nevertheless, Zamalek still retains the aura of its past because it is predominantly the upper middle class who live there. But as the city crowds in on itself, every area becomes a possible location to settle one's family.

Immigration from Egypt to the United States increased in the late 1960s and 1970s because of the political and economic conditions of the time. But perhaps there was another factor. With the advent of television and the increased number of movie theaters, Egyptians began to have access to American shows and movies. What they saw on the screen were people living in large homes with manicured lawns. It must have triggered images of the villas in their own country that had remained out of their grasp. Perhaps they thought that in America they would be more accessible. Today, the cycle seems to continue as American shows gain popularity. In the early 1990s, it was *Knots Landing* that emptied the city streets on Thursday evenings as everyone rushed home to watch the ongoing American saga, slightly censored for Egyptian television.

I remember teaching a class at the American University in Cairo and talking about the problem of homelessness in the United States. The students looked at me bewildered. "America is so rich," they said, "How could anyone be homeless?" I tried to explain and gave reasons and statistics to prove the facts of my statement. They seemed to understand, yet somehow I felt guilty, as if I had taken something beautiful from them. Afterwards, working with the students on their papers, I sat next to a young woman who looked at me and nervously asserted, "But everyone in America, they live like people on *Dallas,* right?" As we continue to export our TV shows, our movies, our music, we perpetuate an image of utopia that instills that desire to leave one's homeland, believing that life's luxuries are handed out once you set foot in America. One poster depicting immigration from 1903 stated, "All those who enter here leave despair behind" (Chermayeff, Wasserman, Shapiro 1991, 24). Perhaps the names that America acquired in other countries are the most revealing. In the early 1900s, America was known as the "golden land" to Eastern European Jews, the "golden nest" to Finns, and the "golden mountain" to the Chinese (Chermayeff, Wasserman, Shapiro 1991, 24). For so many people, we are still the place where streets are paved with gold. Perhaps that is why when the housekeeper asked about life in America for her son who wants to immigrate, I could only say life is hard in America. Maybe I am trying to strike some balance between hope and illusion.

The Marriott and Other Restaurants

A few days after our arrival, we went to the Marriott Hotel in Zamalek for lunch. Originally built as a palace, it is now an impressive and beautiful hotel that overlooks the Nile. There are several indoor restaurants as well as the garden restaurant which serve excellent food offering a mix of Egyptian, American, and French cuisine. Yasmine ordered a hamburger and ate it with great relish, claiming it was the best hamburger ever. Celine too ate her french fries happily. They had found a familiar taste, one that had crossed the ocean with them. With its ideal outdoor setting among the gracefully designed gardens, the outdoor restaurant provides a welcome reprieve from the dust and crowds that border its gates. However, the only ones who can afford this restaurant are the foreigners and the upper class, two groups of people who are perhaps quite similar. The upper class who frequent the Marriott are marked by their access to the West, the English and French that highlight their sentences, most likely learned at the International schools, and their fashionable clothes, probably bought on trips overseas and in the upscale boutiques of Cairo. Chatting easily over their drinks and food, occasionally pulling out a cell phone, they are a stark contrast to the population just outside the gates of the hotel, those who walk in worn shoes, drab clothes, and with shoulders slightly stooped. Every time we stepped out of the hotel, I was struck by the sharp distinction.

The wealthy and some of the middle class help to sustain the Western businesses that are quickly claiming their territory in Egypt. In the early 1990s there were a handful of Kentucky Fried Chicken and Pizza Hut restaurants that had become quite popular, but there were no McDonalds. When we returned just two years later for a brief visit, over twenty McDonalds restaurants had opened and were a favorite place for children's birthday parties. In 2002, Hardees had arrived and was a top choice for many. The number of McDonalds had also increased, and they had introduced a delivery service. The workers rode motorcycles that could maneuver through the heavy city traffic, and they arrived quickly with your food still warm. Other fast-food restaurants have picked up on the idea, and now the streets are dotted with numerous motorcycles that display restaurant logos.

These fast-food chains have become locations of status and money, buoys on the streets of Cairo that mark class differences reflecting an acceptance of American products. Yet Egypt does not lack its own "fast food." *Ful* (fava beans) and *taamia* (falafel) are a staple of the Egyptian diet, and for those who can afford little else, it is their daily food. Numerous small kiosks sell sandwiches, and *Felfella,* a downtown restaurant, has enhanced the simple meals to make them attractive to foreigners.

As political events escalated in 1990 with the Gulf War and then in 2002 with heightened conflicts between Israel and Palestine, antagonism against the United States grew, and these restaurants became locations of political activism. Restaurants like McDonalds and Pizza Hut were attacked. There are those who argue that these restaurants are the hand of American imperialism reaching into Egypt and must therefore be destroyed. Others plead that we are only hurting ourselves because such restaurants create employment for Egyptians and help the economy. A few months after we returned from Egypt, the Pizza Hut where I had attended a birthday party with my daughter for one of her friends was bombed.

Western Products

Buying groceries in Egypt requires that you go to the butcher shop, the bakery, the fruit and vegetable stall, and the grocer, depending on the particular items you need. There are also large open market areas where many of these products are available side by side. Sometime in the 1980s, larger grocery stores began opening, offering everything in one location. During the three years we had previously spent in Egypt, we used to go to Alfa Market, one of the newer stores in the suburb of Mohandessein. They had some excellent Egyptian items, including great feta cheese and olives. Their shelves were also dotted with a variety of American products from corn flakes to pancake mix to chocolate chip cookies. Each year these products multiplied, taking more room on the store shelves. I was perplexed by the particular items that traveled from the United States becoming available to those Egyptians who could afford them. How could chocolate chip cookies compete with the *ghoraybeh* and *kahk* of the holiday seasons? And who would choose a bowl of corn flakes against a bowl of sweet vermicelli in warm milk?

In the years I taught at the American University in Cairo (AUC), I would discuss imperialism with my students and urge them to think about the economic and political consequences of their purchases. I argued, "Wouldn't buying Egyptian products rather than American ones be better for the Egyptian economy?" Their resistance was adamant. "Why should we buy inferior products? Have you tried Egyptian soap?" they challenged me. I felt outnumbered and knew that when I returned to America, I would not have to live with these choices on a daily basis. I remembered my aunt telling me how during Nasser's regime, when he closed off the country to foreign imports, people longed for anything from the outside. "Even a plastic bag from America had value in those days," she said.

International Schools

At times, people comment that I have a slight British accent. Their observation surprises me and pulls me back to a past I thought I had erased from my tongue. Up to fourth grade in Egypt, I attended the Ramses College for Girls, an English language school that still retained a strong British influence. That is probably where I picked up the accent. I remember little from those early school days. I only know that the English I learned was of little value once we arrived in the States. The quick garbled sounds my ears picked up were a series of high-pitched tones that had no beginning or end. It took six months before I could untangle the sounds to create meaning. Today, those who can afford it send their children to English, French, or German schools. The results of an international education can vary. Almost all the students at AUC come from International schools. Some are well versed in two or three languages and equally knowledgeable of the history and culture that accompanies them. Some seem to have shed their own culture and adopted the full wardrobe of the Western one. Others appear to have mastered no language and exist in a precarious linguistic and cultural crevice.

The British school in Zamalek is highly regarded by everyone. It is architecturally imposing, a tall self-contained building that reveals little of itself to those on the outside. The curriculum immerses the students in British history and culture. The Pakistan International School, which Yasmine attended, also adopts the British curriculum, but it seems to do so in a less rigid manner. It provides an international education but one that is firmly located in the context of Egyptian culture. Stepping Stones, which Celine attended, gave us some insight into the first stages of acquiring a Western-based education in Egypt. It is an English language school, but my assumption was that Arabic would also be spoken, at least among the children. What I learned later is that Arabic was prohibited, and children were reprimanded by the teachers if they were heard speaking it.

The American University in Cairo

In 1990, I walked into the American University in Cairo, searching for the English Department. Entering what I hoped was the correct office, I asked in Arabic if this was the English Department. The secretary gave me a puzzled look, so I explained that I was a new professor from the United States. Her confusion only seemed to increase, and her words stumbled, "You're a professor . . . I didn't expect . . . you're from America." "Yes," I answered this time in English and told her my name. Her features relaxed once I switched to English. "I just didn't expect you to speak Arabic," she said. I explained my background and that seemed to smooth over the situation. But I was to encounter this reaction over and over again at AUC. If I walked into an office to make a request and spoke in English, people were very polite and I could get what I needed, but there was a distance that disturbed me. Their manner of responding to me placed me as a foreigner. If I spoke in Arabic, people were very friendly and I felt included, clearly perceived as one of them. However, I also sensed a diminished respect, perhaps because I did not seem to be sufficiently "westernized," and it was difficult to get whatever I was requesting.

It was not until I met Maggie, who also worked at AUC and became a close friend, that I figured a way out of this linguistic maze. Maggie's life was the mirror image of mine. When she was quite young, Maggie had gone to England with her mother, who was working on a Ph.D. When they returned to Egypt, Maggie was eight years old, the same age I was when I left Egypt. Maggie's words tumbled out in English and Arabic, two simultaneous orchestras that played in harmony. None of her sentences contained only one language. Her mind fetched the word that came first or provided the most precise meaning. As we spoke, I unconsciously began to imitate her, finding that mixing the two languages was as natural as taking a step. In adopting this new "language," I accidentally discovered that it was the key to AUC culture. When I spoke in this mixture of sounds and rhythms, people responded with both respect and familiarity, and I could get what I needed.

In the classroom, I encountered a similar dilemma. While teaching about colonialism, I stumbled over my pronouns: we . . . they . . . us . . . them. I existed on both sides of the divide: the colonizer and the colonized. I found myself tumbling over and losing my footing. In this case, I learned to embrace my shifting pronouns; it was the only way to articulate the complexity of my own position.

For me, AUC is the place where I have felt most at home. East and West confront each other both in the curriculum and in the lives of the students and faculty. I felt closest to my students there whose lives also encompassed Arab and Western culture. Their education, class position, and travel experiences had placed them inside and between both cultures. Together we stood on the seesaw, one foot on each side. The trick was not to balance it but rather to keep it in constant motion.

Cairo University

Cairo University is a huge school that enrolls over 100,000 students. It is a public university with very low fees, and students are admitted based on their test scores. It is one of the places that gives pulse to the city. When we taught at AUC, T. J. always used to say that he wanted to teach at Cairo University. In contrast to AUC, with its Western influences, he felt that he would encounter the real Egypt at Cairo University. Yet when the opportunity came to teach there, he was somewhat apprehensive about teaching at such a large university. Perhaps it was how students perceived him that enabled him to find his footing. On the first day of classes, T. J.'s colleague introduced him to the class. He said good morning in Arabic, then his colleague asked the students where they thought he was from. There were a variety of answers from Egypt to Morocco, but no one said America. When they were told that he was indeed American, they were surprised and had to be convinced. But once the case was made, the barriers began to shift. T. J.'s familiar appearance made it easier for students to respond to him, and it also encouraged them to rethink their images of America.

The influence of American media abroad produces a homogeneous image of the American population, the assumption being that everyone in the United States is white. (Even our housekeeper asked me why I had not dyed my hair blond because, she told me, that is what everyone in America does.) T. J. had grown accustomed to this case of mistaken identity from our previous trip. His myriad conversations with shopkeepers, acquaintances, and colleagues required that he explain his existence against the stereotypes that had traveled across the ocean. But there was always a touch of humor as both he and the other person negotiated their way around history. Once someone told him that, although he did indeed look Egyptian, he was willing to believe that he was an American because his feet were too big.

Since its founding in 1908 as the Egyptian University, Cairo University has always been a hotbed of political activism. The demonstrations and protests that erupt around the country often originate on the Cairo University campus. We seem to have a knack for going to Egypt during political crisis. In 1990 when we first learned that we would be going there, I remember people's positive comments: *How wonderful; What a great experience; You'll have a great time.* Then the Gulf War began. The tone shifted and we heard: *Are you still going? Isn't it going to be danger-*

ous? You've canceled your trip, haven't you? The same thing happened as we prepared for our trip that would begin in January 2002. People responded positively to our news until 9/11 happened and once again the tone shifted.

Politics and Translation

I was glad when we finally stepped off the last plane and stood on solid ground. When we got out of the Cairo airport, I breathed in the night air; I wanted to kneel down and touch the ground. This urge perplexes me; I know it is just dirt that a million feet have stepped on. Now I think of the film *Frontiers of Dreams and Fears* directed by Mai Masri. In one scene, teenagers from two refugee camps, one in Lebanon and one in the Occupied Territories, meet at the border that separates the land. Several of the children in Lebanon reach beneath the wire fence to gather dirt from Palestinian land, filling small paper cups and plastic bottles. The same scene occurs in the novel *The Kite Runner* by Khaled Hosseini. When the father leaves Afghanistan, the last thing he does is bend down to fill a snuffbox with dirt from his homeland. While teaching *Beirut Fragments,* a memoir of the Lebanese Civil War, by Jean Said Makdisi, one of my students in the United Sates questioned Makdisi's decision to remain in Beirut during the war, saying, "Why did she stay? I don't understand why. I would have left." I try to explain why someone stays, even against all odds, how the connection to land can be as strong as blood, a bond that holds us tight. Now in Virginia Yasmine says, "I miss the dust of Egypt," and I know that she too has connected to the land in a way that will continue to pull her back.

Ever since I was a child, I have been placed in the position of cultural and linguistic translator. In America, I was asked, "Does everyone own a camel? What's it like over there? Say something in Arabic," and in Egypt, "What do the houses look like? Are people nice? Say something in English." I learned to translate, to explain, to describe, to create scenes of one culture and reveal them to the other, opening a pathway between the two worlds. This time when we were in Egypt, I was placed in the position of political translator, a role for which I was completely unprepared. People spoke to me honestly, and I could hear the trust in their voice, as well as the expectation that since I had lived in America, I could explain America's actions to them. But I felt inadequate for this task. I do not presume to understand international policy, and, like others, I am limited by what the media chooses to show me. Often, I find it difficult to look beyond individual experience. During every war, I am paralyzed by one image—a family sitting in their house, parents holding their children, unable to protect the ones they love. Perhaps that is because one of my earliest memories is of the Six-Day War between Egypt and Israel in 1967. We were living in Mohandessein, a suburb of Cairo. Although I was only six years old, I remember clearly the voice of the town crier as he walked down the street swaying his lantern and commanding us to turn off our lights. My family sat in a circle holding hands in the dark. The Israeli planes flew overhead, and we could hear the roar of their engines. They went back and forth above the city, searching for lights that would indicate a potential target. One of my uncles, who was a doctor, died in the 1967 war, but his body was never found. I can still recall the sadness of his mother's face, her eyes staring into the distance. She continued to wait and to hope that one day he would return.

Parents in Iraq, Afghanistan, and everywhere else want the same thing I do: to raise their children in safety, to give them every hope for a future. When my first daughter was born in Egypt, my great Aunt Alice said to me, "When you have a child, you can see far, so far into the future." But war destroys that distant vision. The image of America as a land of wealth and opportunity has been shattered for many here. The longing to go to America has been replaced by an anger that comes from feeling betrayed. Arab Americans have faced discrimination in the United States for a long time, but those in the Middle East are often unaware of it. Now, after 9/11, they have heard of the random attacks against Arab Americans, and they feel that there is no place for them in this new land. Their belief in those American ideals has turned to bitterness.

In early April, there were protests held by students at Cairo University, Ain Shams University, and some of the high schools. These protests were in response to the increasing conflict between Israel and Palestine and the response of the United States. One day, when T. J. was scheduled to teach, Cairo University students staged a protest against the United States and Israel. T. J. stood outside with some of his colleagues as they discussed whether or not classes would be held. As the protest expanded, a decision was made to close the university gates, and T. J. was told to leave. Fortunately, his appearance enabled him to walk through the protest safely; the students saw nothing more than another Egyptian professor walking by.

The fear is that the anger against U.S. foreign policy will turn into anger against individual Americans. When there is no productive outlet for that anger, it can lash out against innocent individuals who find themselves caught in a cycle of hatred based simply on their physical appearance. It is what happens when someone chooses to blow up a tour bus, and it is what happened after 9/11.

Back in the United States, I am again asked to be a political translator, and I am no more comfortable with the role. Teaching Arab literature requires teaching a history that is unfamiliar to many American students. Without that knowledge, we are left with stereotypes and "around the world in eighty seconds" on the news. While teaching *Wild Thorns* by Sahar Khalifeh, a story that depicts the conflicts and resistance among Palestinians in the occupied West Bank after the 1967 war, one student asked why someone would become a terrorist. Her desire to understand was apparent, but she could not reach that place where such actions become fathomable. Again, my answers felt inadequate. I talked about the complexity of history, land, identity, a conviction in something greater than oneself. But my attempts were as futile as trying to explain U.S. actions to Egyptians. I have been thrust into a role that disturbs me, yet whether in Egypt or in the United States, it seems I must take it on. As Lisa Suhair Majaj explains, for Arab Americans, "this negotiation of cultures results in a form of split vision: even as we turn one eye to our American context, the other eye is always turned toward the Middle East" (1999, 67). I try to maintain this "split vision" as I struggle to explain and to translate.

Snapshot 1

Walid, the young boy, caught our foreign eye outside the
pastry shop, enticed us with his words in English, shook
our hands, and remembered our children's names. He was
selling plastic bags of no use. We gave him a few pounds,
the next day and the next—till he asked for 20 pounds to
borrow for his sick mother.

We knew better but whether out of guilt or kindness we gave
it to him. And we didn't see him again at his post outside
the pastry store.

Till in front of Hardees, we said hello in response to his
avoidance of our glance. But his courage rose to ask me
how much those sandwiches at Hardees were because they
looked so good. And could he borrow some money?

Snapshot 2

In the supermarket,
a foreign man stands
reading the ingredients
on a can of beans,
wearing a summer galabeya,
clean pressed
in peach and white.

E-mails from Yasmine: February

Dear Aunt Anita,

I like Cairo because it's a big city, and it was cool to see it from the plane. But I learned that I don't have to like everything about it. Example: I hate the cigarette smoke. Today my Dad bought me a Bedouin Doll. I named her Bedilya. Celine has one named Asperigast.
Love, Yasmine

Dear Syreeta,

I am remembering my manners, but Celine is getting a little crazy. We went to the Nadi Gezira Club today and I had a hamburger there and it was yummy. The hamburgers are great in Egypt. One of my favorite places is Beanos. It's a great place for dessert. My favorite is the strawberry tart. I also like the chocolate cake. Walid is a boy who goes to Beanos to sell bags. I think Celine will like your new shampoo that smells like cotton candy. It never snows in Egypt. It's really hot here. I miss having you baby-sit for us.
Love, Yasmine

Dear Grandma,

I'm going to the Pakistan International School in March. We have uniforms there. Green tie, white shirt, green vest, gray pants. That's it! I miss you a lot and love you and Grandpa. For Valentine's Day, we're going to the pyramids.

With much love,

your grand-daughter, Yasmine

Dear Aunt Janet,

I do have a great time here in Egypt. I know "No" in Arabic but I also know a lot more. I'll teach you some when I get back. When my Dad and I took a walk today, we saw a rooster in the road. The bird was being chased by children. Bye for now.

Love, Yasmine

PS from Celine: I love you a whole whole million zillion.

Wind

As the sun sets, the people still don't stop the morning run.
As I watch out my window, I still see the store lights
bursting out with color and price.
The dust and smoke can sometimes go on forever
with swirls and it twists and tangles out the window,
through the street, and up and up all the way.
Then it finally settles.

Yasmine Aida Kaldas Anderson

Yasmine About to Sleep, by Celine Aziza Kaldas Anderson

CeLine

Celine Going to School, by Celine Aziza Kaldas Anderson

Molekhia

I'm certain my first solid food was a bowl of *molekhia* soup mixed with rice and pieces of chicken. It provided a nutritious although rather messy meal. In Egypt, you buy the *molekhia* leaves fresh and whole. I've watched my great Aunt Adele bunch the green leaves together into a tight-fisted roll, then, with a sharp knife or blade, she slices the leaves into thin slivers. Her eyes pinch in concentration, and her hands move with calculated precision as her body bends into each slice. Those tiny bits of leaves become the basis of the soup that almost every Egyptian finds irresistible. Some like to eat it plain, some with rice, and some with pita bread. There is the traditional Egyptian bread *(aysh baladi),* which is made with whole wheat flour and has a coarser texture, and Syrian bread *(aysh shami),* which is made with white flour resulting in thinner loaves. Yasmine acquired a taste for *molekhia* while we were in Egypt, and she still fills her bowl with *molekhia* and rice, always asking for a second helping.

In Middle Eastern grocery stores, you can find packets of frozen *molekhia* already precut. That makes the process much simpler, but getting the consistency just right takes a few attempts. Then you have that subtle flavor of the leaves combined with the tinge of pungent spices.

(Egyptians rarely use exact measurements when they cook. The recipes in this book are my own, and I use approximate amounts for the ingredients. Experiment as you cook until it tastes good to you.)

Molekhia

Molekhia is a soup that is best served with rice and chicken.

> 6–8 cups chicken broth (it's best to make it by boiling a chicken)
> salt
> pepper
> 3–5 cloves of minced garlic
> 2 tablespoons butter or olive oil
> 1 package frozen *molekhia*

Season the chicken broth with salt and pepper.

Fry the garlic in butter or olive oil and add to the broth. Add the frozen *molekhia* to the broth and stir very gently on medium heat until the *molekhia* thaws and blends into the broth. Make sure the *molekhia* stays suspended in the pot and doesn't sink to the bottom.

March 2002

Letter 2: March 2002

Dear Family and Friends,

This morning a layer of dust descended onto the city like a thick fog. My eyes are filmed with gray, and my throat is tight and dry from breathing it in as I walk. We're in the Coptic month of *Amsheer,* known for bringing extra dust to the city. And the erratic heat of March is beginning to sneak in, giving us steamy days that make our necks prickle with sweat.

My parents are visiting. It has been fourteen years since their last trip to Egypt, and it has been twenty-six years since the three of us have been in Egypt at the same time. I'm seeing Egypt through their past and the memory stories that I'm hearing from my relatives. I'm amazed by my family's ability to shrink and expand with the process of immigration and return, always making a circle that clasps all of us in our places. We had one of our famous family outings a few days ago. This time we rented a villa with a garden out in the desert on the Ismalia Road in an area called Ahmad Orabi. The women kept straying into the kitchen, Aunt Samia heating the huge pots of stuffed cabbage and white eggplant, and Aunt Adele making the salad and a hummus dip with enough garlic and red pepper to light up a bonfire. My uncles, Adel, Magdy, and Sarwat, grilled the marinated meat and chicken, being sure to taste it as they went along. (At one point, one of my cousins spotted T. J. sitting by the grill in direct path of the meat, joining in as one of the official tasters.) The children explored the garden, discovering the gazebo and the fish pond. (Celine found a small net and went fishing).

The children took turns playing on the patio swing. At one point, the younger kids, Sandra, Liliane, Caroline, Yasmine, Celine, and Michael, were all swinging on it being pushed by the older Marianne and Mirna. Even Sherine, Nevine, and I got a turn. Those of us with young children spent most of our time chasing after them, snatching bits of conversation with each other along the way. The eldest, Uncle Sobhy and Uncle Fouad, sat in the circle at ease, their turn to be served.

This past week, our student from Hollins, Kristin, was also visiting us. Her first comment on arrival was "I can't believe how Western everything is." She was quick to note the McDonalds and Pizza Huts that crowd the city. We made sure that she got a taste of real Egyptian food, taking her to eat *taamia* (falafel); *kosharee* (rice, pasta, lentils, chick peas, crisp fried onions on top with a spicy tomato sauce); and *fetir* (a round layered bread made with butter and baked in a special oven then eaten with cheese and olives or honey), all of which she thoroughly enjoyed.

Our lives here have evolved a pattern. I take Yasmine to school at eight in the morning, return to get Celine ready and take her in at nine. T. J. goes to Cairo University and the Fulbright office several days a week. I spend my time writing, reading, running errands, and doing laundry. At 2:30, I pick up Yasmine and Celine then return home to help Yasmine with her homework.

T. J. has settled into academic life here. He's beginning to get to know his students and enjoys the teaching. In addition, he has been on several panels that interview people applying for research and teaching grants in the United States. He has also found time to pursue his research on jazz. A few weeks ago, he made his way to the Cairo Jazz Club. Here are some of the observations he wrote:

> The Cairo Jazz Club is an easy place to find. You head over the 26th of July Bridge to Midan Sphinx, take exit 2, jump out of the black and white taxi, negotiate your way through the oncoming traffic and head toward the Nile. My first introduction to Cairo's "premier jazz club" was a dust-covered and unlit neon sign placed above a darkened window. Once you're able to squint through the window and ascertain the

place isn't empty, you begin to wonder where the real entrance is or if yet again, you've misread the advertisement announcing the Cairo Jazz Festival. Perhaps it said February 1960 instead of 2002. You see activity, people getting in and out of cars, young boys skillfully directing automobiles into phantom parking places. It's all an urban jigsaw puzzle, an improvisation of human and machine. Once inside, you notice a group of musicians gathering around the front of the room. You can't see much through the crowd; there's no stage. You can make out the crash cymbals, the neck of a bass guitar and the keyboard player. The band starts. It's mainly fusion. The guitarist is ok, but they all seem to be reading from a chart, hard to tell what improvisation is going on. It all seems so mechanical, the drum beats predictable, the bassist keeping time, the keyboards in occasionally with the complementary arpeggio glitter. They close the first set with "Night in Tunisia," so predictable you recognize all of the changes and chord progression. You figure it's time to go, what with the smoke and the chattering crowd and the people yelling over the cell phones. You're anxious to get out into the Cairo night air.

Yasmine has been attending the Pakistan International School for the past month. Her enthusiasm for learning is a wonderful gift that Community School has given her. She wakes up early every morning with little complaint, and at the end of each day, she tells me, "I had the best day." She takes math, English, science, Arabic, computer, ethics (Muslim children take religion), art, music, and physical education known as games. She's also taking aerobics after school. Recently, she performed in a dance for a Mother's Day celebration and did a super job. Here is what she wrote about her school:

My school in Egypt is very different from Community School. In the morning we have Assembly. One day, the tallest man in the world came to school. He had a head like a boulder. He didn't look very happy. He was chewing gum. Then another guy came and moved his eyebrows and his hat tipped. He made animal noises. And at my school they also had an International Day. They dressed in costumes from their country and had a fashion show. I have a lot of new friends.

Three Americans. Their names are Nora, Nazira, and Lamya. Gregory is my friend and he's from Poland. I have friends from Malawi named Aisha and Fatima. I also have friends from Pakistan named Kenza and Ferial. My class teacher's name is Mrs. Inas. She is the math teacher. I love school very much. My school uniform is a white shirt, green tie, gray pants, and green vest.

Celine is enjoying Stepping Stones and holds her own quite well. For the Mother's Day celebration, she made up a song and told her teacher she wanted to sing it. It was an impressive performance! Here are her thoughts:

At school today I drew a little picture. I play at recess four times. My favorite thing in Stepping Stones is computer time. My teacher's name is Miss Paula. I love her very much. My friends are Yoki, and I love love love Yoki. My other friend is a kid in baby class. The only thing we do together is swing because I speak English and she speaks Arabic. And I sure do love Miss Paula. Miss Paula has short hair and it's black. One time at school I tripped over Nada's foot and a boo boo got on my lip. At karate they start saying *eech eech shee.* And at exercise they jump and open their legs and close them and then they start putting one leg in front of the other and start jumping. And at ballet, the ballet teacher's name is Miss Amal. I miss Virginia.

As for me, I'm comfortable here again, at ease in my mixed identity and finding that the movement from one to the other has become more fluid. Last night my parents organized a family gathering at our apartment. Everyone came, even those who don't often see each other. We estimate that around fifty or sixty people were in our apartment. Yasmine and Celine played with children all variously related to them. The thread that ties them together is now too knotted for me to untangle, so I've told them they are all cousins. Between them, they speak Arabic, French, and English, but they have obviously found some means of communicating. At one point, I saw them all in the bedroom jumping on the bed. I simply requested that they take their shoes off first. We ate well, as I come from a family of marvelously good eaters. From pizza to *fetir*, potato salad to pickled eggplant, ice cream cake to *basboosa*, we ate happily, an occasion to bind us again across the distances and differences that threaten to unravel us.

Love from all of us,

Pauline

Journal Entries

March 8

Fourteen years have passed since my parents' last trip here and six years since the last time T. J. and I visited. It's like a fast-paced novel: jump to the future, and people are older, marriages extend the family, and children stretch the bounds of who we are. We're a family woven by past histories yet the future tugs persistently.

Strange to think what our lives would have been if we had never left. Odd, also, to realize how much my parents have changed, that they might be mistaken for being foreign. Immigration changes the body, the way you move, the way you dress, your facial gestures, and the tone of your complexion. I admire their courage to begin a new life. I would not have been able to do it.

March 16

Saw Uncle Amir, Aunt Nadia and my cousin Usama yesterday. They're living in the Old Cairo house again. Usama's brother, Adham, also came over with his wife, Amal, and their three daughters. I've always liked Old Cairo; perhaps it can best be described as a working-class neighborhood. Here, it's rare to see anyone dressed in stylish Western clothing; some wear galabeyas and others wear simple dresses or pants and shirts. The buildings are mostly two or three stories tall, rectangles with windows and doors like the first pictures of a house a child would draw. There's a constant hum of movement in the streets: people walking, a man guiding a donkey, children chasing each other, a woman selling peanuts from a cart. The life of the neighborhood seeps in and out of the houses as if the walls were permeable. A man yells out the window for his son to come home; a woman catches the attention of someone selling watermelons so she can buy one; a girl releases a basket on a rope down from the balcony with money in it to exchange for roasted corn.

I was so happy to walk back into the house, up the stairs as if I'd never left. They've redone the house, and it looks good. My uncle has upgraded the bathrooms and kitchen, changed the location of a wall, and the old house renews itself, still standing despite having its foundation shaken by the construction of the tall building next door. It still has the same spirit, so tangible I thought I could smell it. We sat in the living room, and for an instant time lapsed and we were all there: my grandparents and my cousins and I when we were children. As Yasmine and Celine began to play with their cousins, Michael and Mariam, and Eustina, Ephrasina, and Elaria, time did lapse—a continuous cycle of generations that eludes death. My aunt fried potatoes in the small kitchen just like my grandmother did when I was a child. They were one of my favorite things to eat like all the kids who started eating them before dinner. Yasmine and Eustina managed to communicate with gestures and created games that the others could join in.

My Uncle Amir told me again about my great-grandfather, whose first name was Kaldas. He lived in Abou Teeg, a town on the outskirts of Asyut, where the only jobs were in agriculture and fabric dyeing. Through a connection with someone, Kaldas managed to get a job in Cairo selling tickets on the streetcars. He had plans for building a house in Cairo and moving his family there. One day Kaldas was involved in an accident on the streetcar. He broke his ribs and ended up in the hospital, where it looked like he wasn't going to make it. But he did get better and eventually won a lawsuit against the company. With the money he got, he was able to build the house in Old Cairo. My great-grandfather on my mother's side, Boulos, managed the actual building of the house. So the house was built by both sides of my family. My father grew up in the house in Old Cairo. My uncle opened a door to a room and said, "This is where your father studied. This is where he put his architect's table when he was in college."

My name connects me intimately to this history. Like every child born in Egypt, my first name is followed by my father's first name then my grandfather's first name then my great-grandfather's first name, and it continues. When we immigrated, we were told that we all had to have the same last name, and my father chose Kaldas to unite us.

Kaldas died in 1967—I was about six years old, but I only vaguely remember an old man with a cane. I wonder what he would think if he knew that his great-grandchildren and great-great-grandchildren have returned from America to the house he built and we have filled it with noise and the voices of new children growing.

March 20

My parents are in Sharm el Shaykh, perhaps swimming in the Red Sea. I won-
der if they remember their last vacation in Egypt before we immigrated when
they went to Sidi Abd el Rahaman, a place with the desert spreading on one side
and the Mediterranean Sea stretching on the other. They are pulled back into the
current of lives that includes them despite their absence and opens circles wide
enough to hold us all.

March 30

On Kristin's last day, we went on a felucca ride down the Nile. The slow breeze made the sailboat drift only slightly along the water. I spoke to our boat captain, about the shifts in wind, the tourists, and the best time for a felucca ride. Kristin looked at me and said, "You always smile when you speak Arabic, even to strangers. People here always smile when they talk." Her comment surprised me, an observation I'd never made. I've been told before that when I speak Arabic, I transform, become a different person. I wonder if we smile because we're still very much an oral culture, because words are what bind us.

Family Excursions: 1993

The three years we spent in Egypt when we taught at the American University in Cairo were marked by several family excursions. We'd meet in Heliopolis across from the Ramses statue, caravan style. Getting out of our cars, we'd greet, kiss on both cheeks, hug, and tell immediate news. The first time, astounded by the space we took up in this crowded city, I tried to count us—almost thirty, but I kept losing track—who was in whose car, how many children in each family. Then I tried to link us into nuclear-type family groups, but deciding who belonged to whom only kept me counting in circles that spiraled into each other. Subsequent outings, I limited myself to keeping track of the cars we traveled in.

Most of our excursions led us to *el-Anater*, at the open mouth of the delta where the fingers of the Nile begin to spread. It's a switch from the gray dust of the road to the green of the public gardens at the entrance. Further in, cottages are reserved for officers in the military. Uncle Sarwat, our family officer, is instructed by Aunt Alice, after consultations with various family members, to rent a cottage on a particular day. Once confirmed, she returns to the phone to determine what each person will bring.

Everyone has arrived. Before it's time to cook the food or follow the children to the play area, we gather in front of the cabin for conversations. Aunt Alice stands next to Eman, who is already sitting, facing the water with her feet resting on another chair to control the swelling from her pregnancy; Rami and Maged tuck themselves into the far end for a private conversation, as Rami blows his cigarette smoke out with an exaggerated whistle; Mona rests her weight on one foot while she talks to Uncle Sobhy who, as the eldest of the family, has been granted the shadiest spot under a tree's branch. A dance configuration held still for a moment.

I follow the pattern we make across this segment of green grass at the river's border. There are empty spots where my parents would have been. Our 1969 immigration has left behind space—I imagine outlines of human figures: my father talking to Uncle Fouad, my mother chatting with Aunt Vicky. Space remains reserved, held at bay, and one could step back through.

What happens when memory pulls us back? Aunt Adele and Uncle Sobhy remember my mother, a little girl spending holidays at their house, perched in the study reading their books; Uncle Fouad remembers high school years shared with my father; Mona remembers our childhood escapades gathering bananas from the tree in the next yard, their weighted branches hanging above our terrace.

What happens to sound that would have been uttered here: to laughter, its half tones carried to the river's edge; to words spoken like crocheted doilies, creating dust patterns through their stitches?

I'm talking to Ashraf as I often do at these outings—the only chance I get to speak with him given his work schedule, six days a week late into the evenings. He is Mona's brother, and I'm told the three of us spent much time together as children. Staring at his face, a smile that opens, I try to excavate some memory—left blank—only I keep listening to the pitch of his voice waiting for a gear to be triggered into movement. Again, I explain GREs, a masters in engineering, suggest schools. He's frustrated working for a foreign company with a salary a third of those with American passports. He thinks about going to America for five years, then coming back with a passport and working in the same company to find a way out of this cycle. I encourage, hesitant. I returned here for retrieval—still, I want a family of my generation in America.

My husband is pronouncing his Arabic words carefully to communicate with Aunt Adele, who calls him Thomas, the T. J. an abbreviation of language she can't untangle. But Thomas, from Toma, from the Bible, she can place and recall. I've watched space form—the way eyes define shape from a silhouette—bodies shifting, tongues slipping on a few words in English. A dance movement reconfigures to introduce another dancer.

I feel immortal here. For once my fear of death dissipates, and I wonder if that fear is born out of the loss of generations that occurs with immigration. The children, Marianne, Christine, Mirna, Youssef, survive the same moment as great Uncle Sobhy, whose age no one can figure. There was Uncle Michel, the eldest of the brothers, whose house opened for family parties that grew spontaneously, another brother I called Uncle Whiskey, and Uncle Ramsy who loved peanuts, to my great-grandmother who bore these eight children, and Eman's child and mine who will be born toward the end of the summer's heat, and my own life that will walk through death to this place.

When I heard that Ashraf and Eman and their daughter Nadine had been accepted for immigration to Canada and that Rami too was applying, I sent them a tour book about Canada. They passed it back and forth—I chose the one with the brightest photographs so they would arrive anticipating a Shakespeare performance on stage, a garden with red and yellow tulips, a marketplace soaked in sun.

Rami called—he is in Toronto living with a friend from childhood. He found a job just two days after arriving at a company owned by an Egyptian. "They told me I'd be the warehouse manager and I thought this is a wonderful thing. They took me to the warehouse and when I asked where are the employees, they said you're it." So he lifts computers wearing a belt to protect his back—but his plans are numerous: apply to graduate school, open his own import-export company, move to Vancouver for the oil business. Rami whose pants were always a bit short and who walked as if stepping on a trampoline, his heels bouncing up, puffing out the cigarette smoke with a turn of his head as if one could blow smoke with a French accent, the same way he punctuated his Arabic with "Qu'est-ce que je veux dire?," a phrase I've missed hearing since his arrival in Canada. I imagined him in France, but he claimed no desire for emigration. He was the only one who could talk of racism, teaching me the word in Arabic.

Rami organized our youth outings. Taking after his mother, Aunt Alice, he rang everyone's phone, coercing us to the same date, even Manal, Mona, and Mira, my cousins on my father's side. Once, after we had exhausted more typical outings, he decided we should rent rowboats on the Nile. We argued for a felucca, bright colored, where we could sit on cushions, let the water float us and the driver steer. But Rami was insistent—a felucca for tourists and old people was no adventure. Passing the men along the Nile Corniche who cried out "felucca cheap," he went down some steps to where a man sat quietly with his family and negotiated our rental. Rami took the oars of one boat and Maged, his cousin, took the other, and they rowed us into the Nile. They raced while we joked about tipping over and "whoever drinks from the waters of the Nile will return to Egypt" or catching the disease, bilharzia. Only a palm's length away, the blue-green water stirred its waves.

Ashraf, Eman, and their daughter, Nadine, will arrive in Toronto soon. Ashraf is Rami's cousin so it's good they'll be in the same place. And Rami told me that Mariam, Maged's sister, is coming to Chicago with her husband—she won the immigration lottery. Within arm's distance, they will all be here. To imagine seeing them, my daughter and Nadine, the same age, crossing languages. Perhaps we will come together to celebrate Christmas on the 7th of January. Again, I will hear Ashraf's voice, sectioned on this side of the globe.

Aunt Alice says she will wait for Rami to get settled then arrive. She makes plans, asking if her framed paper sculptures and silk paintings are likely to sell. Will Ashraf bring Aunt Vicky and Mona? Will Maged follow Mariam? I'm counting again—who's left. What spaces hollowed out will remain—the oldest generation? Maged who vows he will not leave? A dance configures around stretches of absence.

A recurring dream: Egypt is only a distance away. I get in the car, drive for a few hours over a cracked mud landscape to reach there. I travel back and forth often, go whenever I want. When I wake, I am startled by the twelve-hour flight, the expense, the measure of time that passes between each return. And who will wait at the airport, what houses will open for us? For my children, what will Egypt be: my husband threw their umbilical chords in the Nile willing the tide to return them. My mother says when she returns, she feels like a stranger and can no longer decipher the streets downtown, once a map in the lines of her palm. As a child living in Maadi, she would circle around on her bicycle as if the streets were her own design. Now she can't locate her sister-in-law's house or the house she grew up where she would sit on the balcony, stretching her eye's vision across the Nile.

I need to stop counting, trust the way sand wind travels through to sounds spoken in tapping rhythms. Where place and memory come from, I imagine us standing at the mouth of the delta. A dance configuration sifting our steps.

March Reflection

IMMIGRATION AND RETURN

When I try to draw distinctions between Arab and Western cultures for my students, I explain how Western culture focuses on the individual while Arab culture focuses on the community. I paint a picture of my extended family in Egypt, tell them that the aunt I feel closest to is actually my great grandmother's sister's daughter. That is how wide the circle goes. Perhaps one of the most difficult aspects of immigration is the way that circle shrinks. There is a sense of isolation that comes with immigration; maybe that is why so many immigrants reach back to bring more family members. When I returned in 1990 and found my place within my family, that split between past and present began to heal itself.

Our family has learned to shrink and expand with immigration. This time, with our arrival and my parents' arrival, the circle grew wider. Being with people who have known you since you were born gives you a sense of security, of belonging. Those people know you more than you know yourself, and their memories extend beyond your own. Being with my family makes me feel that I can reach far back, pull the past around to the present and know it will extend to the future. When we immigrated, the faces and voices of my relatives receded, blurring in my memory, and the effort to recall became too painful.

For many immigrants, the feeling of displacement leads them to look to their homeland as a means of discovering the foundation of their identity. In *Becoming American,* a collection of essays by immigrant women, edited by Meri Nana-Ama Danquah, the struggle for identity is often marked by a return to homeland. These writers describe their visits to their homelands as the turning point in understanding their identity in the new world. In "Secret Latina at Large," by Veronica Chambers, the author is unable to locate herself in any of the available categories because she is both black and Panamanian. During her trip to Panama, she discovers that she is part of a group of people with both a name and a history. She describes the experience as a transformation, "In Panama, I went from being a lone black girl with a curious Latin heritage to being part of the *Latinegro* tribe or the *Afro-Antillianos,* as we are officially called" (2000, 26). When she returns to America, her newfound sense of identity enables her to straddle the inadequate categories of cultural definition in the United States and to confront those who claim that her identity is insufficient. For several of the authors in *Becoming American,* the return to their homelands allows them to retrieve a part of themselves, making them feel whole and connected across time and distance with others. They achieve their American identity only after they have returned to their origins, finding their place within the community that propelled them into the world.

In the past ten years, three of my cousins have immigrated, two to Canada and one to the United States. Those who are still in Egypt also talk of the possibility of leaving. Their frustration at the lack of opportunities and their desire to be in an environment that would enable them to grow is tangible. These feelings are particularly heightened because they are Coptic Christians. As Egypt's population increases and the economy worsens, it seems that opportunities for Copts only continue to decrease. Yet I am still amazed at their courage as they consider packing their belongings in a few suitcases and leaving everything that is familiar to take the risk of beginning their lives again.

When I teach immigrant literature in the United States, the focus is on the lives of those who immigrate, their assimilation, their struggle to adapt to a new environment, their sense of loss. Returning to Egypt, I saw the other side of the mirror: the effect immigration has on those who stay. The gaps in the family are tangible, like sitting in a room with empty chairs inhabited by ghosts. My family's visit filled those chairs, and the words and laughter that erupted was a return to life. It is perhaps hardest for those who stay; the loss is more palpable. There is nothing new to distract them and they live daily with what is absent: the sound of a person's voice, the shoulder they leaned on, the one they confided in. So often it is the older generation that remains and they lose the pleasure of watching and helping the next generation grow: those who immigrate lose the past and those who stay lose the future. Our family struggles to bond across the time and distance of immigration.

Snapshot 3

A curtain unfolds—
a woman wearing a housedress, her arms soft with flesh,
hair adjusted into curlers
and her husband, belly tucked into an undershirt,
a stream of baldness in his hair.
In their bedroom, they pick up clothes strewn on a chair,
wipe a layer of dust from the dresser—
Their evening suspended through an open window.

Snapshot 4

Next to a six-story building waiting
for the finishing touches of construction,
there is a makeshift home:
a tent with rooftop covered in gray canopy,
in front a cactus plant and a woman
wearing an orange scarf on her head.

E-mails from Yasmine: March

Dear Aunt Janet,

I'll tell everyone that you said hello and love them. And for Valentine's Day, we went to the Giza and Saquarra Pyramids. The desert was really hot. I sat on a camel but it wasn't very fun because the camel kept leaning back and forth and so did I. We rode on horses and that was really fun. My horse was beautiful and I named her White Snow. She really trusted me, and I trusted her too. My favorite part was climbing the Queen's Pyramid. I miss you very much.
Love, Yasmine

Dear Grandma,

I miss you a lot. When you talk about the cardinal and the daffodil, I wish I could be there to see it. I can't wait for Spring either. I don't really have a favorite season because when it's winter I like summer and when it's summer I like winter. When it's fall I like spring and when it's spring I like fall.

Today we went to Coptic Cairo. It was full of old churches and things. We touched a glass picture and put our hand to our heart and then we could have blessings. I also liked praying with candles. And there was a big huge chandelier.

Me and Momma have finished the third book of Harry Potter, *The Prisoner of Azkaban!* Daddy just finished the first chapter of it, but he read the first two with me. I read the third book all by myself. And the fourth book is very fat. I'm going to read it by myself too.

Give Grandpa my love.

Yasmine

PS from Celine: I love you Grandma. I miss you very very much. And I already saw the pyramids. I miss you with a smiley face and I want to tell you I love you. From Celine.

Dear Aunt Anita,

I've never been to a wedding anniversary but I bet it's cool. School is really great. The tallest man in the world came. He didn't look very happy. He was chewing gum. He may be the tallest man in the world but he is not the most punctual. I really miss you a lot. I have many friends.

Celine is doing good. Sending e-mails is pretty fun. I go to a restaurant called the Marriott and have a super duper doubleooper hamburger. I'll keep sending e-mails.

Hugs and kisses,

Yasmine

PS from Celine: I love you a whole whole lot. Tell Kalei and Nina I miss them very much and I'm waiting to play school with them. Love, Celine.

My Friend Yoki, by Celine Aziza Kaldas Anderson

A Girl in the Desert with Her Horse, by Celine Aziza Kaldas Anderson

Kosharee

There is a small restaurant in Mohandessein that my cousin Maged took us to when we first lived in Egypt. It is called El Omda and, although there are a few items on the menu, it is really known for its *kosharee.* If you catch the staff on a good day, you'll see one of the servers tossing the rice and lentil mixture into the air and catching it with perfect balance right into the bowl, not a grain lost. *Kosharee* is a wonderful mix of rice, brown lentils, a little bit of small pasta topped with thin crisp fried onions. Then you pour on it a tomato sauce that varies in its spiciness. Whenever my Aunt Alice asks me what I'd like to eat at her house, I request her *kosharee.* I'm not sure what her secret is, but the flavor leaves a tangy taste on my tongue that I continue to relish later. She always makes enough to feed the whole family and anyone else who might drop by. We sit around her apartment, some of us on the floor, in the chairs, at the table, each person with a heaped bowl that entices with its varied colors and flavors.

It's easy to find all the ingredients for *kosharee* in America. *Kosharee* seems easy to make, but I still have trouble getting it just right. It's an ongoing experiment. I'm not sure mine will ever be as good as Aunt Alice's, but I'll keep trying.

Kosharee

Rice

(Make sure the rice doesn't get mushy.)

> 1 cup rice
> 2 cups water
> salt
> 1 tablespoon butter

> Stir the rice and butter until rice is golden, then add the water and simmer covered until done.

Lentils

(The lentils are best when they're cooked but still firm.)

> 1 cup brown lentils
> water

> Put the lentils on low heat, adding more water only when it is necessary. Cook until done but still firm.

Pasta

(Use a small size pasta like elbow pasta.)

> 1 cup pasta
> water
> salt

> Boil the pasta until cooked, and then drain.

Onions

(It is very important that the onions end up thin and crispy.)

> 2–3 onions
> vegetable oil

Cut the onions into very thin slices. Deep fry them in the oil. Let them get to a dark brown color. Take them out and put them on paper towels until they become crispy.

Tomato Sauce
(You can make this sauce as spicy as you like by adding more red pepper.)

1 small chopped onion
3–5 cloves garlic, chopped
1 14 oz. can tomato sauce
1 teaspoon coriander
olive oil
$^1/_8$ to $^1/_4$ cup vinegar
salt and pepper
red pepper (optional)

Fry onion and garlic in oil, then add coriander. Stir in tomato sauce. (You can add some water if necessary.) Add vinegar, salt, and pepper to taste. Stir over medium heat for a few minutes.

Mixing and Serving
Toss the rice and lentils together. Put some of the rice and lentil mixture in a bowl. Add a small helping of pasta on top. Then add the onions. Pour some tomato sauce on top.

April 2002

Letter 3: April 2002

Dear Family and Friends,

Our lives here have become intertwined with the lives of others, connecting us to the intricate web that weaves together the seventy million people who live in Egypt, fifteen million of whom are in Cairo, a city that still feels like a small town where everyone knows everyone else.

Nagah is our housekeeper. She comes twice a week and patiently cleans up the apartment, wiping the dust that can reaccumulate in less than an hour, and putting our abundant papers into neat piles. Nagah is in her thirties, a petite, slender woman full of curiosity. She has asked me to explain everything from coffee filters to pine nuts. And our home has introduced her to a few new things. She drank her first beer by accident, thinking it was a soda since she can't read. Nagah has three sons. After being married for sixteen years, her husband married another woman and sold the house they had bought together, all without telling her. When she started working for us, she was trying to get a divorce and to get her share from the sale of the house. Her husband was still making demands on her, insisting that she give him the money she earned and saying he didn't want to divorce her. One morning, she showed up breathless at our door to say she was getting divorced but her husband wouldn't pay the court fee. I was happy to pay it for her. Her battle to get her share of the money from the house continues.

Nageh is our doorman. (T. J. has had a hard time differentiating between the two names: Nageh, the doorman, and Nagah, the housekeeper. The distinction is natural for me, but his confusion helps me to understand why, in America, I continue to have difficulty differentiating between names like Janice and Janet.) Nageh watches the building, makes sure the elevator is working, and runs various errands for the tenants. He lives in a small room under the stairs on the bottom floor where he seems to have little more than a black-and-white TV. He is an avid fan of soccer so it's easy to find him when there is a game going on. Nageh has a lot of energy and an easy smile. He can always find the right light bulbs for us and gives us advance warning when the water will be cut off. And he always knows who is at home and who has gone out. Last week we found out that he was on vacation. A young man, Ayman, was filling in for him. He showed up at our door trying to deliver a carton of bottled water that he thought we had ordered. I talked to Nageh when he returned and found out that he had been to Aswan, which is in the southern part of Egypt, to visit his wife, son, and seven-month-old daughter.

Gehad is our cook. He comes on Mondays and cooks about six or seven dishes in a matter of a few hours that last us the rest of the week. He is an amazing luxury for us. And, unlike the cook we had last time we were here, he doesn't soak everything in oil. Gehad is in his late twenties, young and very thin for someone who does so much cooking. He has just finished fulfilling his military requirement and is now trying to find a regular job. His hard work began at a young age when he had to leave school after junior high because his father died and he had to help support his siblings. He knows where to buy the best groceries and there is no doubt that he makes the best pickled herring. Occasionally, Nagah and Gehad come on the same day. We're beginning to suspect that Nagah is sweet on Gehad. It could be an interesting romance.

Ibrahim is someone we knew the last time we were here. He is indispensable, and so we quickly tracked him down. I call him the Sam's Club of Egypt. He can get you anything you want from beer and American whiskey to bottled water and paper towels—all in bulk. It's useless to argue with him over the price of things. He can add faster than a calculator, although I recently discovered that he can't read. He is a true entrepreneur. Last time we were here, he was making his deliveries on his bicycle. He became so useful to the expatriates living here that a few of the embassies got together and bought him a car. And now his son helps him out. Ibrahim is the only person I've seen who looks younger now than he did eight years ago.

Hanna is a friend of my family and possibly a distant relative of one of my uncles. He drives a taxi, and so we often call on him when we have day-long excursions or a lot of errands. Hanna has five children. One of his daughters got married and had three children, but her husband died, so now Hanna helps with the care of his grandchildren. Unlike most Egyptians, Hanna is always on time. And he always has a smile on his face even when he's been waiting for us in the hot sun for several hours.

Amr is another taxi driver that we stumbled upon one day. His great advantage is that he has a mobile phone so we can call him when we decide to do things on the spur of the moment. He has a regular full-time job as a driver for the *al-Ahram* newspaper. Unlike most taxi drivers who are curious and want to know everything about you, even when they're just taking you for a quick trip, Amr keeps a professional distance. He asks no questions and reveals little about himself.

T. J. always says, "Everyone has a story." This is certainly true in Egypt. At times I switch my gaze and turn to look at us from the outside—catching a taxi, walking on the street—and if I were a stranger, I would wonder what our story was and how we would tell it.

Love from all of us,

Pauline

Journal Entries

April 5

Our friends from New York, Steve, Catherine, and their daughter, Alyssa, left last night. Their visit was fun and got us out and doing things. Still, I'm glad they're safely on their way home. With the protests going on and the rise of anti-American feelings, I began to feel apprehensive and keenly aware of their physical appearance and how others might perceive them. There was a protest going on one day when we were driving back from a tourist site. Our cab driver, Hanna, positioned the taxi in the middle lane, camouflaging our friends, fearful that the anger of the protestors might spill over.

I don't worry about us in the same way. We all melt into the scenery like chameleons. I worry about the violence and destruction that surrounds us. T. J. says if everyone went to a school like the Pakistan International School, there would be no wars. When the possibility of war would arise, you would think of the boy or girl you went to school with from that country, and you wouldn't want to fight them. Despite our wealth, we are so isolated in the United States. As hard as it is, it's good to have left America for a while, to turn our heads and look from a different direction.

April 13

I'm restless, in some ways bored, eager to go back. Because I'm not working, there's less structure to my days. Yet the bit of time I have just seems to disintegrate. Between the housekeeper, the cook, errands, and laundry, there's no stretch of time left. And the heat has begun. Yesterday, at the outdoor concert, Yasmine almost fainted. I find myself thinking more about my life in the States, wanting to settle in, make it more permanent. My cousin Mira and her husband, Emad, are thinking of immigrating, beginning their lives over again. The courage that takes baffles me. I don't think I've ever been a risk taker. I want to examine where I'm landing before I jump.

April Reflection

MAKING ENDS MEET

I grew up in a middle-class family in Egypt in the 1960s. Like other middle-class families at the time, we had several servants. There was a woman who came to do our laundry. She sat on a low stool in front of a large round tub brimming with soapsuds and our clothes swirling in it. By turns, she would pick up an article of clothing and scrub it between her hands, back and forth against the hard part of her palm beneath her thumb. I sat next to her, imitating her actions. When the clothes were clean, she would rinse them out and wring them tight to release every drop of water before hanging them to dry. There was also a young girl who sometimes looked after me. I hated wearing shoes and socks when I was a child, and one afternoon, I must have decided that I had enough of them. So I proceeded to take off the shoes and socks on my feet and throw them out of the living room window. The young girl went outside to retrieve them and put them back on my feet. This went on several more times. Finally, fed up with my game, she pulled plastic bags over the shoes and tied them around my legs to keep them secure. Her resourcefulness had outdone my persistence.

Today, only the wealthy in Egypt can afford to have more than one servant. Most middle-class families, if they are lucky, have one person who comes perhaps once a week or every other week to clean their homes. Even the language has changed. The word "servant," which was used when I was a child, is now considered somewhat derogatory and instead the word "worker" has taken its place. The service sector is a crucial part of Egypt's economy. You can always find someone to perform a task for you. Sometimes, you may not actually want some of those services, like having someone carry your groceries to the car or wash your windshield. But once the service is provided, you have to pay the person. T. J. grew so accustomed to giving people tips that when Yasmine was born, he gave a tip to the hospital clerk who handed him the bill.

In Egypt's economy, everything is negotiable. The taxi meters are outdated so how much you pay depends on the taxi driver's cleverness and your own wisdom. The price varies based on whether you are an Egyptian who is poor, middle-class, or rich, and it changes again if you are a foreigner either living in Egypt or just visiting. Taxi drivers have an uncanny ability for figuring out the economic capabilities of their customers.

Class distinctions often seem marked by those who provide the services and those who can pay for them. This creates a country of entrepreneurs who, regardless of whether they can read or write, find ways to tap into the marketplace. Many of them, like Ibrahim and Gehad, find a niche by working for the expatriate community. Ibrahim's intelligence goes far beyond his lack of education as he buys and sells with greater shrewdness than those in the stock market. Gehad knows not only how to cook but how to interact with foreigners. His professional attitude has contributed as much to his success as his culinary abilities. Every once in a while, Gehad calls us here in the States just to ask about us and see how we are doing.

Many of those who work in the informal service sector have moved to Cairo from more rural areas, like Luxor, Aswan, and Asyut, in hopes of improving their economic condition. Most of the doormen, like Nageh, who work for the millions of apartment buildings throughout the city, have come from such places. They live in a basement apartment or a small room as they keep a watchful eye on the comings and goings of the building. Every tenant pays them a fee at the beginning of each month and occasional tips so they manage to earn more than what they can in their rural villages. Many of them, like Nageh, have families that stay behind while they work in Cairo to provide for them.

I learned a great deal from our housekeeper, Nagah. After her husband married a second wife, Nagah was working to support herself and to raise her three sons. She was also fighting to get a divorce and struggling to keep her family from forcing her to return to their village, where they wanted her to be under their watchful eyes. In the introduction to *Opening the Gates,* the editors, Margot Badran and miriam cooke, talk about "invisible feminism," explaining that at times feminist acts may not be in the public eye but are still taking place in women's private lives (1990, xv). Nagah, who cannot read and write anything besides her own name, epitomizes that invisible feminism as she continues to struggle to gain economic stability and control over her own life.

Just as my students in Egypt were surprised to learn that there are homeless people in America, my students in America are equally surprised to learn that there is not a significant problem with homelessness in Egypt. They expect that in a country with such poverty, many people would lack adequate housing. Our taxi drivers, Hanna and Amr, reflect the sense of responsibility that many feel towards their families. Amr works two jobs to take care of his wife and children. Hanna's daughter and her three children live with him, and he provides for them financially. That is the norm in Egypt. When one member of the family has difficulty, another member takes that person in. When someone's mother or father dies, the other parent goes to live with their children. There are few nursing homes in Egypt, and it is considered a disgrace to put your parents in one. The notion that your parents take care of you when you are young and you take care of them when they are old is an essential cultural value. So although there is poverty in Egypt, the focus on community and family rather than the individual makes it rare to find someone who lives in isolation.

Many of those who work in the service sector are part of the migration from rural to urban areas that continues to expand the population of Cairo. They find a way to work, to raise their children, and to improve their family's future. Many years ago, my own great-grandfather moved from Asyut to Cairo with that same hope and succeeded.

Snapshot 5

A man selling T-shirts
on the path to the sphinx,
Tutenkhamon's gold face
ironed against black:
"T-shirts, two for ten pounds,
my mother make them last night!"

Snapshot 6

A man in gray galabeya,
slender bones bent to sway his body:
"May God keep you and bless you.
Something to help feed my children.
Their mother is sick. I have five children.
Another pound so I can buy a half kilo of meat.
My children haven't touched the taste of meat.
May God keep you and bless you."

E-mails from Yasmine: April

Dear Grandma,

I'm so glad that you have read the first Harry Potter book. I just finished reading the first book of *Anne of Green Gables* and now I'm reading *The Hobbit.*

I've made many new friends. One of them is Aisha and her twin sister Fatima. They're from Malawi. And Rabia—she's from Turkey. And Ferial and Kenza are from Pakistan. Science is really interesting. We learn about rocks and soil.

My favorite painter is Van Gogh. My favorite poet is William Carlos Williams. I've memorized his poem that is called "This is just to say."

I wish I could be there for Grandpa's concert. I bet it's going to be fabulous.

Give my love to Grandpa.

Hugs and kisses,

Yasmine

PS from Celine: Dear Grandma and Grandpa, I miss you a whole whole lot. And I hope when it's my cousins', Kalei and Nina's birthday, they have a wonderful birthday. Love from Celine.

Dear Aunt Janet,

I would love to visit you in your new house. It sounds terrific. I'm doing great. Things in Egypt are doing great. I miss you a hundred billion. Hugs and kisses a million times. I have lots of friends in Egypt and hundreds of family. We have a cook and a cleaner and a *bawab* (door-man). Write back soon and don't stop because I love you.

Yasmine

Dear President Bush,

I'm an American Egyptian. I'm eight years old. I don't think you're acting well in what's going on with Israel and Palestine. You should ask your people what they think is right before you act. We should make peace in the world and we should respect all cultures. I hope that you'll do the right thing. Peace in the world is very important.

Sincerely,

Yasmine Aida Kaldas Anderson

Egypt

Where the Nile River always flows
and the dusty air is always filled with people
and the hot sun shines on the camels
that go through the desert.

Yasmine Aida Kaldas Anderson

An Egyptian Girl, by Celine Aziza Kaldas Anderson

Man in the Kiosk, by Celine Aziza Kaldas Anderson

Ful (Fava Beans)

My family began to suspect that T. J. had some Arab blood in his past when they heard that he was having *ful* for breakfast. It takes a strong Egyptian stomach to breakfast on this heavy bean mixture. *Ful* provides basic nourishment for the poor in Egypt, many of whom can afford little else to feed their families. *Ful* and *falafel* (known as *taamia* in Egypt) are two inexpensive items and, along with Egyptian *baladi* bread, *tahini,* and some vegetables or pickles, they form the basic meal for many people in Egypt. *Ful* can be eaten for breakfast, lunch, or dinner. It's filling and high in protein.

Fava beans are not too difficult to find here. You can find them dried or canned. They're cooked in a variety of ways: some people like them plain or mixed into a salad, and others prefer them as a sandwich. As they cook, the smell fills the house, making your nose twitch and your stomach long for that full bean flavor mixed with olive oil and garlic.

Ful

For dry beans: In a cooking pot, place 2 cups beans and
approximately 6 cups water. Bring to a boil, then cover and
simmer for about 6–8 hours. Keep an eye on them and if the
water gets absorbed, add more hot water. (In Egypt, the beans
are cooked in a pot called a *dammassa,* which is a pear-shaped
pot with a narrow neck and a tight lid.)

For canned beans: Heat fava beans on medium to low heat. Once
the beans are cooked, pour them into a bowl and add the
following ingredients until they taste good:

salt
pepper
red pepper (optional)
cumin
garlic
olive oil
lemon juice

Fava beans can be eaten by themselves or with pita bread. They
make a great sandwich, especially if you add *tahini,* tomatoes,
and onions. You can also mix them into a salad.

May 2002

Letter 4: May 2002

Dear Family and Friends,

As a child, I remember my parents saying that time moved swiftly in America, that you could hardly catch your breath from the speed of life. They claimed that in Egypt each day took its time, the hours drifting with leisure like a stroll along the Nile on a summer evening. My American logic argued that time was a constant, the same everywhere. Yet here I am with days that stretch like the spring breezes and lull us into believing that summer's heat will never descend.

We've been traveling:

T. J. has gone to Minya, a small town in the southern part of Egypt, about three hours from Cairo by train. He went to give two lectures at Minya University, one on modern American poetry and one on jazz in African American poetry. Aside from one annoying sticky fly that circled his face during one of the lectures, he says it went well. Students and professors attended the lectures and seemed genuinely interested in his talks. Later, the chair of the English Department thanked him, noting how interesting and informative his lectures were, especially since students at Minya University don't take any courses in American literature. T. J. then had to wonder if that look of interest was actually the glazed look of puzzlement. However, he seems to have made an impact, since Minya University has now requested that Fulbright send them a professor who specializes in American literature. Another highlight of the trip was that he had the pleasure of meeting the governor of Minya, complete with bodyguards and dark sunglasses, when he had to wrap up one of his lectures quickly because the governor was scheduled to talk to students in the same room. The visit had such an impact on him that he now jokingly claims his family is originally from Minya. To explain his non-Egyptian last name, he can point to the Anderson Concrete Factory that stands in the middle of Minya. Who knows: perhaps his story holds some truth?

In mid-April, T. J., Yasmine, Celine, and I all enjoyed a trip to Sharm el Shaykh, a resort area at the bottom tip of the Sinai Peninsula right on the Red Sea. On one side, out of the desert, a terrain of jagged, sand-colored mountains rise up. On the opposite side, the Red Sea flows as it has for centuries. The water is amazingly beautiful and well known to divers around the world. By swimming just beyond the shallow area, we were able to look under the water and see a reef filled with corals and fish colored in vivid variations of blue and yellow. We began each day with a buffet breakfast that could make you dizzy with its choices: fava beans, falafel, feta cheese, hot and cold cereals, jams, pancakes, custom-made omelets, and an assortment of sweet breads. Then we spent the day swimming either in the sea or the circular hotel pool. The air is clean and the whole area is landscaped with an abundance of palm trees and flowers that vibrate in bright pinks and yellows. Our evenings began with a stroll along the boardwalk to find a restaurant for dinner. Then we wandered along the many streets and alleys brimming with stores selling Pharaonic knickknacks, silver and gold jewelry, and Bedouin handicrafts. I suspect Sharm el Shaykh must be the axis of Egypt's economy since the area attracts numerous tourists from all over the world, primarily Italy, Germany, Russia, and Israel, and the money flows as easily as the water.

This past weekend we traveled to Alexandria. Located in the north of Egypt right on the Mediterranean Sea, this city has recently undergone a remarkable renovation. All along the coast, the sea was pushed back to create a walkway and a large main street, which circles the northern part of the city. They have also recently completed building the library near the site of the ancient Alexandria Library that was destroyed due to a series of fires. An architectural firm from Norway designed the building in the shape of the sun as a symbol of the source of knowledge. It consists of eleven floors, all of which open up onto each other. They've paid attention to all the details, such as chairs with ergonomic backs and desks with nonscratch leather tops. The library facilities include a planetarium and several museums. Situated in the middle of the coastline, the library with its slanting glass façade is visible from all angles. It can hold up to eight million volumes.

The inauguration for the library was scheduled for early May but unfortunately was canceled due to protests over recent events in Palestine. However, the reading on May 1 was still held, and that is what motivated our trip. I was invited as one of eight writers to read at the library that day. It was an all-day event that included a variety of Egyptian and Arab American writers reading poetry, fiction, and drama. I was joined by my friend, Lisa Suhair Majaj, an Arab American writer who now lives in Cyprus. The event felt momentous, linking our present moment to the past and future.

T. J. is now getting ready to finish up the teaching semester at Cairo University. Teaching during the past political events opened an opportunity for him to discuss with his students the relationship between literature, politics, and activism. He has brought in poems that address political events and encouraged students to write down their own thoughts about what is happening now. The result has led to some powerful writing and strengthened the students' connection to literature.

Yasmine has survived her first set of exams and received her first report card. She has done well, and we are proud of her ability to adapt and succeed in this new environment. Soon she will be getting ready for the end of the year exams, another new experience for her. She has now formed strong connections with her cousins, and they continue to play in a language we cannot understand.

Celine became impatient with the "naughty" boys at her school last month and boycotted the place for a while. The absence seems to have restored her strength, and she is now willing to go again. At home she spends most of her time drawing, and now her pictures include palm trees, Egyptian houses, and little girls at the beach.

I continue to weave together the strands of our life here, trying to keep myself grounded in the present so I can enjoy this time without thinking of past losses or future departures. This past Sunday was Coptic Easter and we celebrated with family, going to church on Saturday evening, then going to my aunt's house to break the fast, eating late and staying up until three in the morning. When I asked a very sleepy Celine, barely opening her eyes at the dinner table, what she wanted, she said, "I want a bed and I want to go in it and sleep." We continued our celebrating by going over to an uncle's house on Sunday where there was more food and more family. The day after Easter here is known as *Sham el Nasim*. It's a Pharaonic holiday that celebrates the beginning of spring. Traditionally, everyone goes out to have a picnic. The scarcity of green space doesn't seem to deter most people. However, given the heat and crowds, we decided to invite family over to our house and instead of the hot spring breeze, we enjoyed our cool air conditioning. At the dinner table, half the family ate chicken and stuffed white eggplants and grape leaves; the other half of the family was more daring and enjoyed the traditional fare of *Sham el Nasim:* pickled herring, fresh green onions, and pita bread. I'm thinking that *Sham el Nasim* is a holiday we need to bring back to the United States with us.

Love from all of us,

Pauline

Journal Entries

May 4

After three days in Alexandria with the Mediterranean waves crashing against the shore, we're back again in Cairo. Alexandria's air is cleaner. Someone told me the Mediterranean takes all the pollution out of the city. And the weather is cooler there, even too cold to swim. People seem less tense—the burden on their shoulders lighter. I wonder if living next to the sea soothes the spirit in some way, makes people calmer. The sea curves around Alexandria, frames the city on its north, right up against the main road and buildings so that it feels like another structure integrated into the landscape. When I stepped off the train in Cairo, I felt slapped by the faces—dark, heavy, burdened, the hardness of living each day etched into their features.

May 17

Morning again—Friday and there's no school—but still waking at 6:20. Yasmine is tired of getting up early every day for school. The routine is exhausting her, and I can tell she senses it's time to play more and study less. Here the school year ends with the heightened work and anxiety of exams. At Community School, it winds down and the children do less work and have more fun as the year ends. And although Celine seems to enjoy her days at school, every morning she still asks if she can be absent. She's ready to stay at home, to lose the structure of the school day. I miss working; each day here is loose, nothing to harness it. I need the routine, the daily interaction with people. Perhaps it's always work that makes you feel that you have a right to be somewhere. I didn't realize last time how important the community at the American University in Cairo was, how it kept us occupied and happy. This time, our lives are quieter with the restrictions of children and school.

Shifting Spaces: 1990–1993

When we were living in Egypt the last time, in the early 1990s, we used to walk almost everywhere. We often went to Alfa Market to do our grocery shopping. Alfa Market was a twenty-minute walk away from our Garden City flat, going by Kasr el Aini Hospital, a complex of orange bricks and white cement, where my cousin Mona did her residency. We had gone to visit her one day, our shocked expressions hidden as we watched the patients walking up and down the hallways with no supervision. One man, his head round and balding, wearing a green dressing gown, browsed through a tray of medication. We peeked into the rooms to see patients sitting on the floor sharing the evening meal brought by relatives.

A trespasser coming to ogle the natives. No clear distinctions: *Egyptian—Not Egyptian.* Fear chiming through my body. Safety? By conjuring up those aseptically clean hospitals in the United States, strict regulations. Embracing home. Distancing home.

After the hospital, we pass the Manial Palace, an assortment of villas including King Farouk's hunting lodge. Now a modern five-star hotel where I can run from the pollution and the clothing restrictions—no shorts, nothing sleeveless, and the sun's heat pouring sweat down your back. Could I wear a galabeya, loose to my ankles, designed in flowers, the traditional dress now associated with being lower-class? I wasn't raised into the ease of wearing one. I'd feel disjointed maneuvering through the streets in it.

The Manial Palace Hotel with palm trees caressing a round pool. For forty pounds: spend the day with buffet lunch stretching across four long tables, wearing your bathing suit. No veiled women swimming, long skirts twining their bodies. My body exposed in their stare—the family at the Marsa Matruh beach whispered as I quickly slipped on a loose dress after swimming. Is this my Americanness: the heavy breath of balancing rocks?

An oasis with an arranged jungle of plants cleaning the air so you could forget about coughing up black phlegm, relax on lounge chairs, breathe easily. A space to be with other expatriates, as if I were American.

But in other places, so oddly disjointed. Social gatherings discussing the peculiarities of Egypt and Egyptians, techniques for survival. An American woman living alone complains how fruit and vegetable merchants give her the worst produce when she requests only a quarter of a kilo.

I explain: they don't like to sell less than a kilo. Egyptians live in large households, few people buy so little. Perhaps establish a relationship with a particular merchant.

Her response: a defiant toss of the head. An assertion she has a right to buy as little as she likes.

Then put up with the spoiled produce! But I keep quiet.
Feel the edges of space pressing me.

Not a spokesperson for Egyptian culture. So much I don't know but learning from a different location—an Egyptian, not a foreigner memorizing her lessons. Yet, conversations place me on the dissecting table except, twenty-five years in America, allow my Egyptianness to be overlooked.

Maureen's parties on the roof of her AUC apartment downtown. Overlooking the entire city, pattern of rooftops, rising and falling. The citadel in the distance lit up. The tallest building with the neon *Sport Cola* sign. Closer, a makeshift home on top of a roof, two men talking, a duck, a cat. The city revolving, my arms wide to embrace it.

Looking out over the roofs, Barbara says, "Cairo is just like a big village."

Jolted back.

To travel this distance, be here, live, and still see only what you imagined before you came?

rooftops clamoring for space
night air seeps through a maze
I'm tucked into a refrain of images.

After the Manial Palace, we walk over the Giza bridge. Sometimes in the evening, a bride and groom stop to have their picture taken under a halo of moonlight. The Nile laid out behind them, red and yellow feluccas drifting open sails toward the wind, and the Meridian and Gezira Sheraton hotels creating a landscape of lights over the water.

So many weddings—Adham, Mira, Ashraf. After her wedding, my cousin Mira, who was moving to Asyut with her husband, stood in the bedroom trying to squeeze her twenty pairs of pants, ten belts, thirty scarves, fifteen fancy dresses, along with shoes, skirts and shirts, into two suitcases. I was called upon for American ingenuity, made decisions, assured her Asyut was only an hour flight; she could get the rest later.

My Aunt Amal's apartment in Maadi, up a half-circle of gray cement stairs, was small for her husband, herself, and three daughters: two bedrooms, a dining room, small kitchen, bathroom, and a tiny living room like an entranceway where we usually sat. But the space left behind when I immigrated in 1969 was still there. I neither had to be invited nor ask to step back into it. Even in the middle of summer, heat penetrating the walls, one tiny window in the room, I stayed for hours, forgetting the time.

When Mira called to tell us that her father, only in his fifties, had died suddenly of a heart attack, my breath stalled. I looked at my husband, knew he was remembering Christmas at St. Mary's Church, walking through a maze of cobblestone streets in Old Cairo, where my uncle was a chanter. He was a lawyer by profession but the music of the church was his true passion. I was sitting with my Aunt Amal and her daughters. My husband had to sit on the other side with the men. In the middle of the liturgy, my uncle walked back, took my husband's arm and led him to the front, making a place for him with the other chanters, wearing their white robes with red sashes and gold crosses. He was the tallest among them, but he hummed in the language still new to him as my uncle smiled proudly.

At my aunt's house after the funeral, we felt awkward, not knowing what to say, how to react.

He always greeted us wearing light blue pajamas or undershirt, at home sitting in his chair. With family, there was no embarrassment. How formal: his picture framed in the dining room, wearing his lawyer's suit.

We didn't know what to bring so we brought oranges and peanuts. Emad and Mira and her sister, Manal, laughed at the strange offering and we all stood in the kitchen eating, still able to smile a little.

They pressed clay
Shaped space.

❧

Once over the bridge there is the tall building, plants draping its entrance. The Omam restaurants on the top floor—Japanese, Indian, Italian, Moroccan. Luxuriously decorated and expensive by typical Egyptian standards, a hundred pounds for a meal for two. But we had gone there several times. Our AUC salaries made that possible. Left behind our part-time jobs in Rhode Island, living paycheck to paycheck, gathering our change at the end of the month to buy Chinese food. Arriving in Egypt, we became wealthy.

Our first week in Egypt, a friend took us out. As we walked in the upper class suburb of Mohandessein, a young beggar girl began to follow, trailing my dress (bought in America, orange and green, circles and triangles). Ignore her. Persisted at the edge of my dress, not even asking for money, looking up: as if I were some kind of princess.

Our friend managed to make the girl go away. The sidewalk moving. I looked ahead wishing *to twirl around, catch the girl in my arms, pirouette the air.* Only to descend, and the longing of her vision persists, my creation, indelible.

In our AUC Garden city flat, a plumber came to fix something and brought his son. The young boy, six or seven, stood, transfixed in the living room staring at us. Our friends Maggie and Ayman and their daughter, Tia, were there. We told the boy to follow his father, but he wouldn't budge. Through his eyes, the apartment, magic carpets to ride, bouncing on clouds. We had created the moment of his poverty.

Space crowded
tapestries, rugs, vases piling my mummified corpse

A woman asks where I work.

"I teach at the American University in Cairo."

Replies, "You're not really living in Egypt."

Where was I? Egyptian colleagues. Egyptian students.

AUC in the middle of Tahrir Square, originally one of Khedive Ismail's palaces with delicately carved mashrabiyya windows. The center of the city. The most prestigious university in the country. Job ads specify a preference for AUC graduates. But the first time I step on campus with its manicured lawns, tennis courts, and courtyards with fountains, I wonder if I'm still in America. The students in European clothes, young women wearing miniskirts, young men on a fashion runway in their jeans. I puzzled at how they got through the city streets dressed like that.

Drivers bring them to school, pick them up at the end of the day. Surveying the city from the back window of a car, they don't feel the air tightening around their bodies as they maneuver through the overcrowded city. Where was I, participating in this space of Western images, gaining respect because I had lived in America?

Alfa Market was one flight up in the tall building. A new supermarket like Sunny's and Tamco's. Not a Super Stop & Shop but nevertheless with shopping carts and aisles.

On one side, toys and housewares. Barbie dolls dominating, prices starting at a hundred pounds. Contained in sparkling spaces, an array of paraphernalia.

Young men from Upper Egypt, military duty, holding guns and standing guard in front of embassies, cultural centers. Ten-pound monthly salary. Sometimes clicking the safety at a passing foreigner.

In the food section, products multiplied: Oreo cookies, pancake mix, corn flakes, saltine crackers. I had vowed never to buy any of them but when I got pregnant I was grateful for the saltine crackers.

Alfa Market still sold the olives, feta cheese, and pickles, but instead of being piled in cylinder containers or tucked behind the counter, they were displayed behind the glass case, neatly arranged into patterns of colors delicately sparkling. It was still wise to give the man who sliced your cheese a tip, but he had learned to subdue the sense of urgency.

One day I saw a woman, heels and tailored skirt, with her servant trailing in a dark galabeya, carrying a child, pushing the cart. Where was I? The space between them. *The young girl who took care of me when I was a child—I cried, not understanding why she couldn't come to Alexandria on vacation with us.*

Who would I have been if I had stayed?

So oddly matched these products. *Could I take a box of pancake mix for my partner, dance a waltz to drum beats, an olive at the tip of my tongue?*

Back into the street with our shopping bags, over the bridge trembling with our footsteps. My husband's brown complexion and features identified as Egyptian—"a weight lifted off my back"—not a black male in the suburbs followed by police cars. Nothing to distinguish him. I look like so many other Egyptians. *Horns improvise a discordant melody as we walk, mirage images in a neon lit landscape.*

May Reflection

UNDERSTANDING WHERE WE ARE

When T. J. and I teach in the United States, we try to broaden our students' vision of the world by introducing them to a variety of literature—African American, multicultural, immigrant, African, or Arab. In Egypt, T. J. found himself doing the same thing as his lectures encouraged students to see the world through other lenses. Since our return, we were pleased to learn that a Fulbright scholar in American literature did get assigned to Minya University. It is the stories and poems of others that make our world larger, that stretch our vision so we can see beyond our own experiences. And yet that process can at times be difficult and frustrating. When T. J. introduced his Cairo University students to political writing in American literature, urging them to write down their own political thoughts, some students found the exercise liberating while others questioned why he would encourage them to become politically vocal when there was nothing they could do. They confronted him with a sense of their frustration as individuals who could not counter the actions of stronger nations.

I have watched T. J. redefine himself within his new role at Cairo University. As he decides what to teach and how to reach his new students, his understanding of himself changes. Introducing American literature and African American culture to students who are unfamiliar with American society challenges him to read the literature he teaches from a different perspective. To see a new culture requires that you position yourself in a different place.

I have watched Yasmine and Celine go through the same process. Yasmine has made friends from different countries; she is beginning to recognize that her own identity is a crossroads of cultures. She writes poems that reflect the sounds and smells and textures of her new environment, and within that she places herself in a new location of identity. Celine draws pictures of the children at her school, the boats on the Nile, the pyramids in the desert as she explores her new surroundings. And she begins to draw herself, at school, on the beach, with her friends, creating new locations to define herself. Art, whether literary, visual, or performative, is the way we decipher our world. As recipients and creators of art, we are in constant motion, shifting our perspective of the world and our position in it.

I have repositioned myself within my family, becoming no longer a child but an adult. The rhythm and pattern of family gatherings hold my days together. When I am in America, I call Egypt on holidays and my aunt or cousin says, "Remember when you were here and we spent the holiday together?" But it is more than memory; I am transported to another place. Perhaps as Edwidge Danticat says in "AHA," our shadows can travel so we can be in two places at once. I feel that possibility especially on holidays when I sense that my shadow is in the other country joining the celebration among family. Once we have relocated ourselves, we can no longer exist in just one place.

Snapshot 7

Bus sways, tilts itself to a stop—
a woman holds an infant, turning his face to the window's light,
a man drops his forehead, holds it against his wrists.
Bus sways, realigns itself to move—
a man grasps the handle, shifts his body's sweat
toward a slipped breeze from half-opened window,
a woman clutches her bundle, settles her weight
toward the pole plastered with holding hands.

Snapshot 8

A woman disembarks at the train station:
her posture grand,
her steps of equal proportion.
The basket on her head is a still figurine
and in her hand
she carries a chicken,
its wings firm in her grasp.

E-mails from Yasmine: May

Dear Syreeta,

 Don't feel bad about being jealous because it's natural. I'm so glad you're going to take pictures for me at the Community School Strawberry Festival. I wish I didn't have to miss it. I miss you a lot. By the way, you said you missed me two times in your letter. But that is just as much as I miss you. I can't wait until I get back and you can give me explosions.

 I hope my Daddy and Mommy get me a present from Egypt so I can have an Egyptian present for my birthday.

 Write back soon.

Yasmine

Dear Everybody at Community School,

 I miss you all very much. I'm glad you liked my postcard. Computer at my school here isn't very fun. We don't go to the lab often. We usually just sit in our places and write about computers. I'm surprised that some of you got your hair dyed. I'm eager to see how it looks. I just wanted you to know that our karate teacher did not show up, so I'm taking aerobics. It's really fun. My mom said it will be really hot in the summer. I know two girls who are from Pakistan. Their names are Kinza and Ferial. I have two friends from Malawi named Fatima and Aisha. I miss you all a lot. Write back soon.

Love,

Yasmine

Dear Everybody,

How are you doing? I'm great! We're at the Red Sea. We go swimming everyday in the beach and pool. We went on a glass boat and a motor-boat. The sea is very salty. I miss you so so so much.

With love,

Yasmine

The Pyramids, by Celine Aziza Kaldas Anderson

A Girl on a Hammock Drinking Lemonade in the Desert,
by Celine Aziza Kaldas Anderson

Grape Leaves

In the apartment in Mohandessein where I lived as a child, we had a large terrace that was encircled by grapes. The first step in making grape leaves was going out onto the terrace to pick the leaves off the vines. Making grape leaves is time-consuming, but in Egypt, cooking is rarely a solitary act. I remember sitting around the kitchen table with my grandmother, my mother, and my aunt to roll the grape leaves. They taught me how to spread out the stuffing, how to roll the leaf tightly so it wouldn't unravel in the cooking, and how the smaller the grape leaf, the greater the skill of the cook. The pot would fill quickly and soon the aroma seeped through the house tempting me to sneak a grape leaf out of the cooking pot and taste its fresh, green flavor.

Grape leaves have made their way to America. Here I buy the leaves in jars. I'm always amazed at how most Americans will eat just a few of them. In my family, we pile our plates high with them and eat until there is no more left. Now I usually make them only on holidays. But I love opening the refrigerator to find the cover of the pot tipped over, evidence that my daughter Celine couldn't resist having just one more.

Grape Leaves

Grape leaves are best served with a yogurt salad: just mix plain yogurt, salt, chopped garlic, ground mint, and thinly sliced cucumbers.

> 1 large jar or 2 small jars of grape leaves
> 1 pound ground beef or lamb
> 2 cups uncooked rice
> 3 tablespoons butter, softened
> 1 large onion, chopped
> Salt and pepper

Place chopped onion in a large bowl, add salt and pepper, and rub together. Add uncooked rice, meat, and butter, and mix well.

Rinse grape leaves very well. Boil leaves, a small bunch at a time, in a large pot half full of water for about 10 minutes. Remove leaves and drain.

Place one leaf on a plate, flat with stem sticking up. Cut off the stem. Place a thin strip of stuffing across the top part of the leaf. Turn the top of the leaf over the stuffing, then turn in the sides and roll tightly.

Arrange stuffed leaves in a pot in rows on top of each other. You can sprinkle some of the stems in the pot. Add the water that the leaves were boiled in to the pot so it's about $2/_3$ full. Let the water come to a boil, then simmer, covered, for about 1 hour. Add about 1 tablespoon lemon juice at the end.

June 2002

Letter 5: June 2002

Dear Family and Friends,

All along our street, the poinciana trees have bloomed with flaming orange flowers. One tree after the next creates a bright canopy that shields us from the heat and dust.

We have just returned from a week in Cyprus, where we were visiting our good friends Lisa, Andreas, and their daughter, Nadia. Cyprus is a beautiful country, and there the streets are lined with olive trees. On one side there is the Mediterranean, clear and blue. The beach is clean and comfortable, dotted with just a couple of restaurants where you can take a break from the waves and sun to eat souvlaki, which comes in great varieties (beef, chicken, spiced ground meat, grilled *halloumi* cheese). On the other side are the mountains, and tucked inside them are villages with narrow winding roads and small whitewashed houses on either side. Our friends led us through one village to a restaurant known for their walnuts, nothing ordinary, but walnuts off the tree, whole, with their green shell soaked in syrup. We had a picnic in the mountains where the air was cool, relieving us from the city's heat. After we ate, we filled bottles with mountain water straight from the source. Andreas's family has a small farm, filled with an abundance of trees and vegetables: olives, lemons, oranges, figs, pomegranates, grapes, watermelon, squash, tomatoes, cucumbers. His father is up at 6:00 A.M. every morning and begins his day by working on the farm for several hours. When we went to his parents' house for lunch, his mother had cooked everything that day with vegetables freshly picked from the farm in the morning, including stuffed squash flowers, something we had never seen before, and they were delicious.

Our friends live in Nicosia, a city that is divided between the Turkish and Greek sides of Cyprus. Downtown, we were able to go right up to part of the wall that divides the two sides, known as the Green Line. It is guarded by United Nations soldiers, and we were able to look through openings in the wall to see the Turkish side.

T. J. liked Cyprus so much he didn't want to return to Egypt, and I even heard him say something about retiring there! He has finished the term at Cairo University and is now focusing on trying to find out what he can about jazz in Egypt. The rest of the time, he attempts to hide out from the heat. These summer days are difficult when the normal temperature is above one hundred degrees mixed with pollution and humidity.

Yasmine finished her school year with splash and flourish. First there was a week and a half of exams: each morning there was a final exam for an hour and a half then she came home to spend the rest of the day studying for the next one. Her stamina held out, and she did remarkably well. Her favorite subject was science. After exams, there were two weeks of rehearsals for the annual show. In hundred-degree weather, the kids practiced their dances and songs outside over and over. But I must admit it was worth it: the show was superb with a lot of energy and color. Yasmine participated in the hat dance and the aerobics dance as well as several songs. She did a great job, and I think she'll remember those dances for a long time to come.

Celine has also finished school, ending with picture day, where she got her picture taken wearing a graduation gown. Now she spends most of her time creating art. For a while, she focused on noses and each little girl she drew had a different kind of nose. Then there was salami art, a complicated process of tearing pieces of toilet paper, wetting them, coloring them with a green marker, and then molding them into different shapes. This culminated in an exhibit and we were all invited to the opening. While on the beach in Cyprus, she had a momentary breakdown when she couldn't find any paper on which to draw. Fortunately, there were napkins at the restaurant. These days her constant refrain is "I miss Virginia."

I have now reached the point where everything has become familiar and ordinary again, and it's hard to remember that I have another life elsewhere. My body has adjusted so I can even go out in the middle of the day at the height of the heat. The broken sidewalks, the crowds, and the puzzle of traffic are the fabric of my daily life. I look around our now full apartment, anticipating the packing ritual. But before I make any progress on that, there are more friends and family to visit and a bit more time to allow myself to be immersed here.

Last night we went to the Citadel to watch a performance of music and dervish dancing. The show began with ten men standing next to each other playing various instruments: the *rebaba* (a two-stringed instrument played with a bow), *nai* (a reed flute), *mizmar* (a horn that requires an amazing amount of breath to blow), *tabla*s (drums, including some that are flat and round like tambourines), and cymbals. Each of the musicians had his own style expressed in facial gestures and body movements (one almost laughing as he played, another smiling as if with a hidden secret, a third curving his body into his instrument). Then, taking turns, one musician at a time stepped forward in front of the line to begin a solo on his instrument. As the musician became immersed in his solo, the others joined him, sometimes with one note on one instrument or two musicians together or the whole group, creating a musical conversation. The *tabla* player crackled with his drum, beating out a variation of rhythmic notes that it seemed impossible they originated from the same instrument. The most entrancing musician was the man playing the cymbals. He played with a large set on each hand, creating sounds that seemed to speak with their tone and articulation. But his instrument was both the cymbals and his body as he danced while he played, enticing the audience with his sensual movements.

This was followed by two Whirling Dervish dances, a dance that is connected to spirituality and prayer. The dancers are all men and they twirl and twirl, beginning slowly, then picking up speed, then slowing again, then picking up a frenzied speed before finally slowing to a stop.

Their costumes consist of layers of wide multicolored skirts that fan out and circle with them as they twirl. They untie one, circling it at their head so they become an hourglass shape of moving colors, then they turn it above their heads with a single hand until they catch it, fold it, and hand it to one of the other performers, all the while their bodies never stop twirling. Behind the dancers were the row of musicians, and one singer who sang religious songs. One dervish dancer was circled by about six men who also danced, playing tambourines and urging him on. This dancer went on twirling for over a half hour. In the other dervish dance, there were three dancers twirling, the middle one moving counterclockwise and the two on either side moving clockwise. They became a whirlwind of mesmerizing movements and colors. Watching the dance is hypnotic, pulling you into a trance that captivates the eye.

With love from all of us,

Pauline

Journal Entries

June 1

Morning—drinking coffee—6:30—my birthday again in Egypt. How many birthdays have I had here and if I count them, will it tell me anything? Yesterday, Mira and Emad were over, and I was trying to convince them to come to the States. What right do I have to tell them to take a step like that, as if I had some answer?

And that picture of us the night before we immigrated—a whole family—everyone in one place. All those who would be born in Egypt were already there. Mira on her grandfather's lap at six months old. Who would have known that her mother and her older sister would immigrate and she and her oldest sister would stay? And all of the adults, all of them, except my grandparents and Uncle Amir, would leave. The family scattered like split seeds. Here I am years later trying to gather us again—reposition us in one picture, in one place.

Perhaps I want my cousin to come only to affirm my own sense of rightness in being in America, like my parents who brought over one sibling after the next. Is it only an attempt to retrieve our own loss? At times, I feel whole, secure, solid; other times, the ground cracks under my feet.

June 29

We have just returned from a week in Cyprus where we stayed with our friends Lisa and Andreas. They live in Nicosia and we also went to Episkopi, where Andreas's family has a small apartment close to the sea. It was the garden behind the apartment and Andreas's family farm that impressed me the most, reminding me how much I'd like to have a garden of my own. It made me nostalgic for the garden we had in Egypt when I was growing up: the guava tree, the mango tree, the grape arbor. In Roanoke, all my plants are in pots, and T. J. keeps urging me to put them in the ground. I've been waiting until we settle down to start a real garden—perhaps it's time.

June Reflection

AUTHENTICITY AND INFLUENCE

I had never heard of America until my parents told me we were moving there. My world was home, family, school, outings to the pyramids, vacations in Alexandria. That was as far as my vision could stretch. Like many children, my understanding of place was bound by what I could see and where I could go. The plane that took me to America forced me to redraw that map, to recognize immediately and abruptly that the world's boundaries were far greater than what I had experienced. As a child, I could never have imagined that I would have family and friends in so many countries.

Today, a wall still exists between the Greek and Turkish sides of Cyprus, and Israel is building a wall along the West Bank. Such walls have marked our history, creating divisions that limit our vision. Although politically motivated, they also create cultural boundaries.

As an immigrant who came here as a child, I am part of what Rubén Rumbaut called the "one-and-a-half" generation (quoted in Firmat 1994, 4). Emigrating as children, this generation is situated between those who emigrate as adults and those who are born in America. The question of authenticity is one that plagues many of us who cannot define ourselves with a single term. I have watched some of my students struggle with the same issues as they try to make sense of how blood, location, and language become signifiers of identity. Reading *The Woman Warrior* by Maxine Hong Kingston made my Chinese American students ask one another, "Are you more Chinese if you grow up in China-town and go to Chinese school than if you grow up in the suburbs?" Our nation asks similar questions as homogeneity and heterogeneity continue to confront each other under the banner of national identity.

Our daughter Yasmine rejects the label some put on her, telling her she is half African American and half Egyptian. "How can you be half anything?" she asks rhetorically. She claims an identity made of two wholes so that she can be all Egyptian and all African American at the same time. That question of blood and identity has plagued the United States since the beginning. To maintain a clear distinction between blacks and whites, which was essential to slavery, even the smallest amount of black blood meant you were black and could therefore be treated as legally inferior. Today, to claim officially a Native American identity, you have to prove that you have a certain "degree of Indian blood." It seems we might divide ourselves into oblivion. Yasmine's math makes more sense: each part of you equals a whole.

I grew up listening to Abd el Halim Hafez, Farid el Atrash, and Om Kalthoum, the icons of Egyptian music. Their voices rang clear from radios, TVs, and movie theatres; they were the heroes of Arab culture. Their songs lingered in people's ears, long songs that spoke of the desperation and longing of love. In an Om Kalthoum concert, the audience would respond to Om Kalthoum's magnetic voice, urging her to stretch her words until each song became an infinite sound that seeped beyond the barriers of the concert hall. To please her audience, Om Kalthoum would repeat phrases, varying them each time, so that a song would last much longer than intended. Today, Egyptian musicians like Mohamed Mounir, Amr Diab, and Hisham Abbas utilize the beat of Western music, combining a duality of sound to create songs that can speak to a generation that struggles with the influence of Western culture.

The audience watching the dervish performance was made up of Egyptians and non-Egyptians, an opportunity for a sharing of culture that offers the possibility of learning and influence. The Whirling Dervish dance is spiritually rooted. As the dance progresses, the turns become more dynamic and vibrant, moving the dancer into a trancelike state. The music urges the dancer to continue until he achieves a kind of spiritual ecstasy. This dance, which was originally part of a religious ceremony, has now become an entertaining performance. It can be watched in places ranging from the Citadel, where we saw it, to the tour boats that drift along the Nile offering a full buffet along with a show featuring a belly dancer and a dervish dancer. I cannot judge the authenticity of the performance we watched, but I can say that it far superseded the one available on the tour boats that is performed by only one dancer. The communal quality of the Citadel performance highlighted the interaction of the musicians and dancers. It also utilized the improvisational techniques, which allow for one musician to be featured while still maintaining the integrity of the group.

I wonder what happens when dervish dancing and music are performed in the United States? In what way does the performance transform? Does it become less authentic? The same questions must be asked when Western music travels to other countries. What happens when an art form like jazz, which is deeply rooted in the political, historical, and cultural experiences of African Americans, gets transported to other locations? How can musicians in other countries express that same music? Perhaps what disappointed T. J. in the jazz concert he described is that there was nothing new, only the predictability of an art form being imitated. Because jazz has been influenced by various types of music, it may be possible for Egyptian musicians to take it in a new direction. However, the issue of authenticity can often stagnate the potential of artistic influence, which must ultimately lead to innovation rather than imitation. It is perhaps not so different from the creation of identity especially for those whose lives encompass various cultural strands.

Snapshot 9

Her speech sprinkles English and French
like scattered powdered sugar on cookies
falling into indented designs.

Snapshot 10

Like a true Arab
he dips his fingers in the pot,
plucks a grape leaf,
drops it in his mouth—
a morsel of taste.

E-mails from Yasmine: June

Dear Grandma,

I can't wait to see Jeff and Julianne's baby. My favorite thing to eat here are the pastries. They're really good. I like baklava and lady's eyelashes best. The favorite thing I've seen here are the pyramids. I liked climbing the Queen's Pyramid. The spirituals you mentioned sound very interesting. Here there's a call to prayer for the Muslims. I think it's kind of pretty. I miss you and grandpa a whole lot and I can't wait to see you again. I miss roller skating. I don't know how to ice skate. I tried once but it didn't work. Write back soon.

Love,

Yasmine

Dear Syreeta,

I wish I could have seen you graduate from Hollins. I would love to see you in that costume. Celine graduated from her school too. Annual Day at my school was terrific. I was in three dances. We had to go up and change real quick. I was in a hat dance, an aerobics dance, and a final sports dance.

Hugs and kisses and explosions.

Yasmine

PS from Celine: Syreeta, I miss you a million zillion billion killion times. Love Celine.

Dusty City

The Nile sparkles on the city.
Palm tree shadows I see.
The boats glide against the river
knocking waves onto my forehead.
I see people out fishing and someday
I know that I will be one of those people.
It's afternoon and I'm looking forward to dinner.
The breeze knocks against my head.
The noise and the rush of the dusty city
remind me of my imagination.

Yasmine Aida Kaldas Anderson

The Belly Dancer, by Celine Aziza Kaldas Anderson

Noses, by Celine Aziza Kaldas Anderson

Baklava

Egyptians love sweets. The streets in Cairo are filled with a variety of pastry shops. Some display two sides: one with French pastries topped with fruit, chocolate, or cream that taste as good as they look and the other with the syrupy sweetness of Middle Eastern pastries. One of my favorite trips as a child was the one we made to Groppi for my birthday cake. These were elaborate cakes, sumptuous in their size and elegant in their decorations. Groppi, in the middle of downtown, was known for the artists and writers who frequented it. It still retains some of its old charm. I grew up eating the common Egyptian pastries: baklava, *basboosa,* and *konafa. Basboosa* is made with a type of farina that gives it an almost nutty texture. *Konafa* is made with shredded wheat that is packed tightly into a pan. Between the layers of wheat, there is a nut mixture or sometimes a sweet cream. And of course, like the other pastries, there is the syrup poured on top. My paternal grandfather loved my mother's *konafa* so much, he would arrive at our house each Friday carrying the ingredients and wait until my mother made it for him.

Baklava has become popular here, and Americans don't seem to have any problem adapting their taste buds to its extra sweetness. I learned how to make baklava from my mother. Although it takes a long time to make, it's worth it. I love taking the tray out of the oven, seeing the rows of diamonds tinged with gold, and hearing the sizzle as I pour the syrup over it.

Baklava

Syrup

(It's best to make the syrup first since it has to be cold when it's poured over the baklava right when it comes out of the oven.)

2½ cups sugar
1¼ cups water
1 tablespoon rose water
1 teaspoon lemon juice

Boil the water and sugar in a saucepan. When it is clear, add the rose water and lemon juice. Let boil just a little longer. Be sure the syrup cools completely before the baklava is ready.

Stuffing

(Nuts were scarce in Egypt when I was a child. Usually we made baklava with walnuts because they were easier to get and not as expensive as pistachios. It tastes good either way.)

1½ pounds of either walnuts or pistachios
3 tablespoons melted unsalted butter
4 tablespoons sugar
1 tablespoon rose water

Chop the nuts so they're about the size of small beads. Add the butter, sugar, and rose water and mix well.

Baklava

(It takes a while to do this part, and it's important not to stop in the middle, otherwise the phyllo will dry out.)

2 16-oz. packages of phyllo
1 pound of unsalted butter

Heat the butter and remove the top foamy layer.
Grease an 11 x 17 inch pan. Layer the phyllo one sheet at a time,

brushing butter on every other sheet. Be sure to cover the entire sheet with the butter.

When you've used one package of phyllo, put the nut mixture on top of the last layer of phyllo, which should have no butter on it. Spread out the nut mixture evenly.

Continue layering with the next package of phyllo, again brushing butter on every other sheet. Don't put butter on the top layer.

Cut straight lines through the pastry approximately every inch down the length of the pan. Then, in the other direction, cut diagonal lines approximately every inch. The result should be rows of diamond shapes. After cutting, brush the top layer with butter.

Cook in preheated oven at 325° on a high shelf for about one hour. The top layer should be slightly browned. Take it out of the oven and immediately pour the cold syrup over it. Let it sit and cool before trying to take it out of the pan.

July 2002

Letter 6: July 2002

Dear Family and Friends,

There is a new building being constructed at the school across the street from us. I've been watching it the last couple of months since piles of sand and concrete appeared in late May. The children simply incorporated the construction materials into their playground, climbing and running around them. The foundation took the longest and for a while it wasn't clear what they were doing. Then quickly the steel beams rose and took the shape of what will probably be another classroom building. Once I felt the floor of our apartment move, and T. J. said it was probably the crane across the street causing a vibration in our building.

There are six suitcases firmly packed and standing in our hallway. Yet our apartment still seems full. I'm not sure what is in those bags, and I don't know how we managed to accumulate so much. Now it's clear that we will need at least one more suitcase. We've started giving things away: the kitchen things to our cook, Gehad; household items to our housekeeper, Nagah; some kids' clothes to our taxi driver, Amr, who I just learned has a three-year-old daughter; and a few odds and ends to my family. We're leaving a trail behind us like grains of sand as if we could follow it back.

We've been eager to leave. The summer heat and pollution have worn us out, and Yasmine and Celine have suffered from particularly bad stomach upsets. Yet a few days ago, we were taking a felucca ride on the Nile in the evening as the breeze was picking up and the sun was setting. T. J. and I looked at each other, and without words we both knew that we would miss being here, that despite all the annoyances, we would find ourselves longing again to feel the energy and spirit of this place and to be part of it.

Our ritual of good-byes has begun, and each day someone in my family has invited us so we can spend a little more time together before we leave. I try to hold back any picture of the future: how big these children will be the next time I see them, whether or not this older aunt or uncle will still be here the next time I come back. Returning at these long intervals is like reading a book quickly, where there are only a few pages between birth and adulthood, between youth and old age. I feel caught in those pages, unable to stop their speed; all I can do is slow them down for the short period that I'm here.

In just a few days, we will leave this place that we have called home for the last six months and return to another place we call home. It will be a long time before any of us understands how this experience has transformed us. We hope that our desire to give Yasmine and Celine a larger vision of the world has succeeded. At any rate, they have left their mark. Celine lost her first tooth in Egypt and Yasmine lost a tooth in Cyprus while eating a souvlaki. Both the Egyptian and Cypriot tooth fairies arrived bearing gifts.

We've all learned a great deal here. T. J. has once again learned to respond to the shifting perceptions of his identity, and he has succeeded in teaching across cultures. Yasmine has learned how to make friends from all over the world and how to survive final exams. Celine has learned how to make friends who speak a different language and how to put up with the rambunctious boys at school. I have once again learned how to walk the broken sidewalks of Egypt and how to light a gas stove with a match.

We will miss a great deal. T. J. will miss smoking the water pipe known as *shisha* and walking the streets with that sense of anonymity like a grasshopper on a leaf. Yasmine will miss eating all the sweet pastries and seeing her Egyptian identity reflected around her. Celine will miss eating grape leaves almost everyday and being spoiled by her extended family who has come to know her for the first time. I will miss the sense of belonging within my family and the feel of Arabic on my tongue that has now become fluent so no one comments on my accent.

As we sift through our complicated feelings about being here and now leaving, it is Celine who firmly calls us back home, asking each day, "Are we going back to Virginia today?" The first two words she put together as a child were "Come back," and I've always known that she would be able to do what I never could: point to a place and unequivocally claim it as home. And so with her urging, the last suitcase will be packed, the last good-byes said, and we will return once again to renew our lives.

I will end with a poem Yasmine recently wrote. Perhaps this trip will be the most significant for her. When we arrived in Egypt six months ago, she was eight and a half years old, exactly the same age I was when I immigrated to the United States. And so she can best express who we are now.

WHO I AM

A dark purple sky with flying seabirds.
Sharm el Shaykh and Cyprus have a lovely swimming place.
Dark faces, black hair are my relatives
with a whole bunch of Oklahoma in between.
Some beating of drums
Some Pharaohs
and some American cheese
are who I am.

Yasmine Aida Kaldas Anderson

Looking forward to seeing all of you,
Pauline

Journal Entry

July 10

All these years I've been haunted by loss. This return to homeland has finally freed me. Immigrants return to their native land to discover their original identities, to claim a right to their ethnicity, to embrace a homeland of at least a spiritual belonging. But I have come back this time to unexpectedly find myself laying claim to my present life in the United States, and with it the undefined future for myself and the generations to follow: who my children will marry; what ethnic identity my grandchildren will claim; and how distant generations will create themselves anew. My Egyptian identity will dissipate, perhaps only a memory for the generations to come. But this no longer frightens me; no longer is it marked by what will be lost but by what will be gained. I'm releasing the strands of loss that I have held for all these years.

An Evening Sweep: 1998

We had just moved to Roanoke, Virginia, and I was sweeping at night again. Once the sun's light has dimmed enough so I can see only myself reflected in the living room windows, I begin to notice the bits of food under the dining room table, and they irritate me. So I bring out my broom and dustpan and sweep them up.

In our old apartment in Binghamton, New York, my mother came to visit once and, seeing me drag out the vacuum cleaner one evening, she gasped, "Don't you know, you shouldn't sweep at night." But then she caught her breath back and said, "Oh, but you want to move." She was right. I thought I had overcome the old Egyptian superstition: if you sweep (or vacuum—we had to adjust it to include the new technology once we arrived in America) at night, then you will move. I had grown up with this belief like a thumbprint on my forehead, along with all the other superstitions that managed to cross the ocean with us: if your left hand itches, you will get money; if your feet itch, you will travel; if you have a sudden, choking cough then someone is speaking about you; if your eye flutters then something bad is about to happen—but that last one was complicated—it depends on which eye and it differs for each person, so you have to figure it out on your own. There were others. My mother claimed they were silly, part of the old world that she wanted to leave behind, but she paid attention to them as diligently as music students practice their scales.

Apparently I had only reversed the sweeping one, attempting to manipulate it to my own desires by sweeping at night so that we would move. In Egypt, moving is not always a good thing. Finding an apartment in a crowded city like Cairo is difficult. So, you live with your parents until you marry, then, if you're lucky and if you've saved enough money, you move into your own apartment and stay there permanently. The reasons to move are not usually due to good fortune: a spouse's death or immigration—and whether that's good or bad, well, it depends on if you're looking at it from the eye of the one who is immigrating or the one who is staying behind.

My mother let me sweep. We were finishing up our graduate degrees at last, and T. J. was on the job market. Obviously, the goal was to find a teaching position and move elsewhere. Well, I'm not sure I like the elsewhere—in this case Roanoke, Virginia—and that's why I'm sweeping again. But I'm beginning to worry about ever liking a place well enough to once again bow obedience to the superstition. Unintentionally, perhaps due to having children, I've acquired the desire for the American dream and want that piece of land with a house and yard, to set down a claim and draw a boundary around what I can call my own. America moves too much, sometimes like a mudslide. I long for the way we stay put in Egypt, how I can always return and know each aunt and uncle will be in the same house, and I can follow the turns of the streets, trust the familiar smells, and keep mark by the same kiosks to find my way there.

Everyone assured me that my older daughter, Yasmine, who was five, would adjust easily to the move from Binghamton to Roanoke, that I shouldn't impose upon her my own grief from immigrating when I was eight. So I pulled my history back, read the tips for helping children move, and comforted her questions—yes, she would miss her friends, but there would be new friends to make, and of course we would go back and visit. Yet, despite all my preparation, she found my past on her own.

Lying on the rug in our living room in Virginia, she told me, "I'm dreaming."

"What are you dreaming?" I asked.

"I'm dreaming that I'm here in Virginia," she answered.

"And what happens when you wake up?" I questioned.

"I'll be back in my old house in Binghamton," she said.

My nerves chimed like when someone stumbles on your hiding place. How could she have found it? For years after our arrival, I would close my eyes to make America a dream that I could wake from and find myself back in Egypt with life about to continue as it was.

In Egypt, we lived in the suburb of Mohandessein in an apartment on the first floor of a two-story villa. Inside, the hallway led to my parents' room. On one side, there was my grandmother's and aunt's room and on the other side my father's studio with his architect's tilted table and the small bed where I slept. It had a shiny green cover that felt like satin as I rubbed my hands over it. Our kitchen had a table in the middle, and that is where my grandmother bent over to roll the dough when she made the *kahk,* the *ghoraybeh,* and the petit four cookies on holidays and where we sat together when we rolled grape leaves. The kitchen opened to the terrace and garden where Tumbuz, the neighborhood cat, ran off with the chicken he stole off the kitchen counter. Our salon was a sacred room for formal occasions with deep green and gold furniture and my grandmother's piano. The actual family room is where we usually sat—we'd be sitting there in hot summer's heat fanning ourselves and each person would push me away if I tried to sit too close, resisting the stickiness of another body.

My friend Maggie and her family recently moved from Egypt to England. She writes to me about Tia, her daughter: "Tia was telling me this week that she cannot remember what her bedroom in Egypt looks like anymore and that she misses it, and every now and again she asks me what did our house look like, I cannot remember." What will my own daughter remember of her first home? Is her mind already distilling images so some fade and some accent into relief? It's her best friend she cries for the most, asking if she can go to her house so sincerely I can believe it's possible. I watch the creation of her loss, an empty tube inside her body to keep the space of what she once held. And I listen to my one-year old daughter chant the names of friends left behind and wonder how memory retrieves loss at this younger age.

Since I've been in America, I've never gone anywhere with the intention of staying. Moving to go to school or to work temporarily, I've always planned my departure before my arrival. Yet I long to stay in one place. I wanted my children to be born and raised in the same house, to give them the permanence of familiarity that I lost. My parents' immigration led them to Boston, and they have stayed there since, their moves only from one house to another. I envy my mother's belief that Boston is the best place to live. Most older immigrants stay put; finding themselves in America at last, there seems no need to move beyond where they place their first step. Or maybe it's possible to call up the will for such a move only once. But those of us who come younger or are born here, we seem to hop like fleas trying to catch some new desire.

I know it's not so much about place as it is about familiarity, that going to the same store each day to buy a loaf of bread is more the definition of home than anything else. That it's the repetition of daily habits that my daughter misses the most: playing hide and seek with her friend next door, riding the carousel in the park near our house, being greeted with the same chant of voices in her classroom. For me, it's driving down the same street to the supermarket that puts me at ease and learning a new set of directions that most disrupts me. In a new place, I spend hours poring over the city map trailing the street lines, memorizing how they connect.

My left eye has been fluttering ever since we arrived in Virginia. But I can't remember whether it's my good-luck eye or my bad-luck one. I can never keep track, and when I ask my mother which eye is which, she reminds me that it differs for each person.

I know there are other superstitions, ones that didn't cross the ocean. Maybe it's best not to recover them. I'll work with what I have, sweeping my floor each evening until we reach home.

July Reflection

LANDSCAPES

The movie *Double Happiness,* directed by Mina Shum, explores the life of a Chinese family living in Canada, focusing on the dilemmas faced by their older daughter. In the final scene, as the daughter is leaving her parents' home, knowing that this means she will be disowned, her mother says, "Now who knows what will happen?" The daughter responds, "Maybe I like not knowing." Whereas the mother wants her daughter to follow a clearly marked path based on set cultural values, the daughter is unafraid of creating a path that is uniquely her own. In trying to please her parents, the daughter becomes burdened with their cultural expectations to a point that threatens to destroy her; her decision to move away from her parents releases that cultural burden, freeing her to redefine herself. In that last scene, the mother's comment expresses her fear of what will be lost while the daughter's response focuses on the possibility of what will be gained.

My first trip to Egypt as an adult in 1990 allowed me to reclaim a sense of who I was, to own the knowledge of my cultural identity, and to create a unified identity rather than the fragmented one that had been thrust on me by my American experience. The second trip allowed me to release the sense of loss that comes with the immigrant experience. Perhaps that is because I returned this time with my two daughters. I could no longer look in the direction of the past, but had to turn my gaze towards the future that my children will create.

A few weeks ago, while having dinner at a friend's house, in the middle of appetizers and a pleasant conversation, Yasmine tugged at my shoulder. With sadness painted across her face, she said, "I miss Egypt, I miss Aunt Alice, I miss my cousins, I miss eating *molekhia*." There is nothing I can do; this sense of loss is now deeply imbedded in her. Still, the next day I make *molekhia* for dinner and that helps to soothe her.

It has been two years since we returned from Egypt, but sometimes Celine will begin to tell us a story about something that happened. Her story is in the present tense, but slowly we figure out she is talking about things that happened at Stepping Stones. We interrupt her, point out this was in Egypt and in the past. Our observation is irrelevant to her, and she continues. Egypt and Virginia, Stepping Stones and Community School, the past and the present: she collapses them and places them in front of her in a seamless pattern.

From Yasmine, I have learned it is possible to create wholeness. Her poem, which ends letter six, weaves together the various strands of physical appearance, geography, music, history, and food into one poem that can hold us.

From Celine, I have learned that at some point you must choose a place to claim as your home, a place to locate yourself even as your shadow travels, even as loss fills your body, and even as nostalgia tugs at your memory.

When we finally landed in Roanoke, after a long trip that included engine problems and a bumpy plane ride that popped us out of our seats, we were, needless to say, quite relieved. We were returning to a place that had become even more familiar after being away from it. The children were looking forward to going back to Community School, T. J. and I were looking forward to returning to our jobs and friends, and we were all eager to be back in our own home. The same things that had given us a sense of belonging in Egypt—school, work, home—were here waiting for us.

Our initial move to Roanoke had been a difficult one, both because we had grown so attached to upstate New York, where we had lived for the past five years and built a community of friends and also because it involved a move from North to South. As an immigrant, I tended to see America as a whole with regional differences receding into the background. Our move to Roanoke brought those regional differences to the forefront. Even before we got there, my attempts to speak to people on the phone as we made plans for our move were filled with frustration. Somehow I could not get the information I needed. I felt ill equipped, as if I had missed a step in the directions for putting together a piece of furniture that comes in a flat box with planks of wood and a bag of nails. Things did not improve much after our move; it seemed the only people I could get along with were other transplants from the North. I was a bit resentful. It had been hard enough to adjust to America, and now I was faced with another cultural adjustment.

Teaching graduate students from the Roanoke area helped me to begin to confront and peel away my own prejudices toward the South that I had unknowingly picked up by virtue of living up north. Still, it was little things that tripped me up, like the way people waved to each other as they drove and the way it took so long to get anything done. When we returned from Egypt, something fell in place; it was as if my hands had been on the wrong piano keys. Finally I figured out that all I had to do was move them over to get the right note. I puzzled over this. Why did it suddenly seem so easy, so natural? Slowly, I realized that perhaps the American South and Egypt were not so different from each other. If you saw someone you knew, it was not good enough to say a quick "hi" and keep on walking; you needed to stop and chat for a few minutes. If I wanted something, it was always better to go and ask in person, beginning with a genuine conversation before I made my request. Unlike the North, where I had learned that quick and to the point was the appropriate behavior, it seemed that here human interaction was more valued than efficiency and speed. Like Egypt, what you could accomplish was not simply based on your own abilities but on your relationships with other people.

The importance of oral communication, which Kristin had picked up on when she said people in Egypt always smile when they talk, was true in Virginia, too. What initially appeared to me as simply a veneer of friendliness went further than that; it was an acknowledgment of sharing space and an awareness of the dependency we have on each other. When our kids run into the peanut store downtown to get some samples, the owners know them and do not mind the small handful they take. When our daughter goes to the food court for lunch and orders from the Japanese booth, the owner greets her and tells her to say hello to us. Roanoke is a city, and yet every time we go downtown, we run into people we know; like Cairo, it is a city that acts like a small town.

I had separated America and Egypt so much in my mind, drawing a distinct cultural line, that I had missed the obvious signals in front of me when we arrived here. This was a culture that was not so unfamiliar. When we first settled here, the Blue Ridge Mountains that surround the valley of Roanoke felt gigantic and looming. They seemed to move, closing in on me. I had never paid much attention to landscape before, to how it can affect you and make you feel connected or disconnected to the place where you live. Without realizing it, I had grown accustomed to the rolling mountains and numerous lakes in upstate New York, and the movement in that landscape made me feel at ease. People in the United States move from one place to another so frequently, it never occurred to me that one could become connected to a particular physical environment. But in Roanoke, I began to hear people speak of the mountains with a sense of reverence and attachment. My first environment had been the water of the Mediterranean and the sand of the desert. They marked the boundaries of my childhood and helped me to understand my place in the world. When we left Egypt and returned to Roanoke, slowly I began to see the beauty of the mountains, the way they cradled the valley and the way their shape and color shifted with the seasons. Perhaps the mountains that surround Roanoke are not so different from the sea that embraces the coast of Alexandria or the desert that frames the city of Cairo.

Snapshot 11

Inside:
Heads bent over scratched desks, pencils gripped,
tight-lipped worship of an indeterminate future.
Outside:
Parents line the sidewalk in front of the school,
keeping vigil, muttering prayers to reach their children.

Snapshot 12

In the evening when I walk,

the second security guard on the block is always singing.

Tonight, his hands are cuffed around his mouth,

his voice resonates against the green kiosk.

To shelter him from rain and sun's heat,

his tenor voice wraps around the words calling.

E-mails from Yasmine: July

Dear Grandma,

I wish I could have gone to Italy with you and grandpa. I miss your pecan and cranberry pie. I miss the stories you read to me at night. For Mom's birthday, I got her some pretend little chickens on a chain with a bell at the bottom. I miss you a million zillion billion times. I'm going to start reading *The Diary of Anne Frank* next week and I have four Archie comics. For my birthday, I want a turtle and Addy's school desk.

Lots of love to you and grandpa,

Yasmine

Dear Syreeta,

We'll be back in Roanoke late on July 22. Don't forget to come visit us.

Love, Yasmine

The Tooth Fairy in Egypt, by Celine Aziza Kaldas Anderson

My Own Home, I Miss It So Much, by Celine Aziza Kaldas Anderson

Kahk

My childhood memories of Christmas and Easter are not filled with the anticipation of presents, but with the taste of cookies dissolving on my tongue like sugar cubes. I would wake up to plates piled high with *kahk, ghoraybeh,* and petit four cookies. I don't know when the women in my family made them, and I never questioned the hours it must have taken them. Since we fasted before Easter and Christmas, eating no meat or dairy products, this taste of butter and sweetness was intricately linked with the holidays. *Kahk* was my favorite, and I ate one after the other, the cookies crumbling into my mouth and the powdered sugar sprinkling on my clothes.

Making *kahk* was not one of my mother's specialties, and so we rarely had them after we came to the United States. One Christmas, I decided that I would make *kahk.* After the disappointment of the first batch, I proceeded to call up female relatives and friends asking each of them for their *kahk* recipe. Because Egyptians don't use precise measurements when they cook, these recipes were filled with "a little of this and little of that" and "twice as much of this as that." I experimented with one recipe after the next, and my family obliged by tasting each batch. Finally, I came up with my own recipe, and my family assures me that it's perfect.

Kahk

$4^1/_2$ to 5 cups flour
4 sticks (1 pound) unsalted butter
1 package yeast
1 teaspoon sugar
dash of salt
$^1/_2$ cup warm water
powdered sugar
chopped walnuts

Pour flour into a large bowl. Melt the butter until it fully boils, then remove the top foamy layer. Pour the butter slowly on top of the flour. Add a dash of salt. Knead mixture until all ingredients are mixed well.

Mix yeast, sugar, and water in a cup. Let the mixture sit long enough to rise. Add the yeast to the dough and continue kneading. Cover mixture with a towel and put in a warm place for 15 minutes.

Take a small bit of the mixture and roll into a ball about the size of a walnut. Poke a whole into the ball and fill with a few pieces of walnuts. Close up the ball and flatten out. Design the top with a fork (normally a tweezerlike utensil called a *monash* is used to make designs on the *kahk*).

Put *kahk* in an ungreased pan and cook at 325° on a high shelf for 20–30 minutes.

When *kahk* is completely cooled, sprinkle powdered sugar on top.

Celine's Reflection on Egypt, 2005

The dusty street
The dusty road
No way no how this is gonna change
Or rearrange
Because it's Egypt
The Nile River Arabic
I can sing the alphabet: *alif, beh, teh, theh*
It's the way I like it now
Instead of saying *Adios* or *Ciao*
I say *Ma Salaama*
So say good-bye to you
But not to Egypt
It stays forever
And there's nothing about that I can do.

Celine Aziza Kaldas Anderson

Journal Entry

July 18

Thursday morning—last day—our countdown has ended and tonight we leave: our apartment that we have made a home for the past six months, family that has been a part of our daily lives, friends that our children have made, stores that have become integral to our lives and whose owners know us well.

I wonder if in being here these six months I have transformed the future. Every time I've come, someone soon thereafter has immigrated. The first time it was my cousin Mona, the second time it was my cousins Rami and Ashraf. Who knows what my presence has done without my knowing, tying our futures together.

I will miss my family, speaking and hearing Arabic, the sense of familiarity, and seeing my life from beginning to end, not as fragments to be taped together. But I will not miss the excessive heat of summer, the pollution that is tangible before your eyes, the verbal politics of daily interactions, or the constant giving of tips. And I look forward to the intellectual and artistic energy of the United States—that community that I have made myself a part of. I think I can let go of the past, and hold the thread of my present to pull me ahead. I can look forward to the mystery of my descendants' future.

But enough—now the last bags need to be packed, the last clutter cleared away, the last phone calls made, and the apartment left empty with just a touch of this and that to show we were here, like Yasmine's hat from her dance at school in the living room, my flowers from Mother's Day on the table, T. J.'s coffee mug in the kitchen, and the little box Celine drew on the wall.

Works Cited

Badran, Margot, and miriam cooke. 1990. "Introduction." In *Opening the Gates: A Century of Arab Feminist Writing*, edited by Margot Badran and miriam cooke, xiv-xxxvi. Bloomington: Indiana UP.

Chambers, Veronica. 2000. "Secret Latina at Large." In *Becoming American: Personal Essays by First Generation Immigrant Women*, edited by Meri Nana-Ama Danquah, 21–28. New York: Hyperion.

Chermayeff, Ivan, Fred Wasserman, and Mary J. Shapiro. 1991. *Ellis Island: An Illustrated History of the Immigrant Experience*. New York: Macmillan.

Danticat, Edwidge. 2000. "AHA." In *Becoming American: Personal Essays by First Generation Immigrant Women*, edited by Meri Nana-Ama Danquah, 39–44. New York: Hyperion.

Double Happiness. 1995. Dir. Mina Shum. New Line Studios.

Firmat, Gustavo Perez. 1994. *Life on the Hyphen: The Cuban-American Way*. Univ. of Texas Press.

Frontiers of Dreams and Fears. 2001. Dir. Mai Masri. Arab Film Distribution.

Hosseini, Khaled. 2003. *The Kite Runner*. New York: Riverhead.

Khalifeh, Sahar. 1985. *Wild Thorns*. New York: Interlink.

Kingston, Maxine Hong. 1975. *The Woman Warrior: Memoirs of a Girlhood among Ghosts*. New York: Random.

Majaj, Lisa Suhair. 1999. "New Directions: Arab-American Writing at Century's End." In *Post Gibran: Anthology of New Arab American Writing*, edited by Munir Akash and Khaled Mattawa, 67–77. Syracuse: Syracuse Univ. Press.

Makdisi, Jean Said. 1990. *Beirut Fragments: A War Memoir*. New York: Persea.